Why Most Advice is Wrong

Surendra Shrivastava

Why Most Advice You Hear is Wrong

Surendra Shrivastava

Published by Surendra Shrivastava, 2024.

While every precaution has been taken in the preparation of this book, the publisher assumes no responsibility for errors or omissions, or for damages resulting from the use of the information contained herein.

WHY MOST ADVICE YOU HEAR IS WRONG

First edition. October 21, 2024.

Copyright © 2024 Surendra Shrivastava.

ISBN: 979-8227040787

Written by Surendra Shrivastava.

Surendra Shrivastava
(Self-Help Author)

TABLE of Contents

CHAPTER 1 2

The Illusion of Expertise 3
Why Popularity Doesn't Equal Wisdom
The Echo Chamber of Bad Advice
Spotting Red Flags in 'Expert' Guidance

CHAPTER 2 2

When Common Sense Isn't So Common 3
Why Passion Alone Won't Pay the Bills
The Problem with "Quick Fixes"
'Advice That Feels Good But Hurts Later

CHAPTER 3 2

Unpacking the Psychology Behind Bad Advice 3
Cognitive Biases: The Invisible Forces Shaping Our Beliefs
Emotional Persuasion: When Advice Plays with Your Feelings
The Power of Storytelling: Good Stories, Bad Lessons

CHAPTER 4 2

Breaking Free from Bad Advice 3
How to Develop a Critical Thinking Mindset
Trusting Your Experience Over Someone Else's Words
Creating Your Own Path: What Works for You

CHAPTER 5 2

The Art of Giving (and Receiving) Better Advice 3
How to Give Advice Without Becoming a Know-It-All
Learning to Receive Advice Without Losing Yourself
The Future of Advice: Learning in the Digital Age

From the Author

DEDICATION

This book is dedicated to those who have journeyed with me through the landscapes of the heart and the mind. Your presence, encouragement, and love have been the guiding light in my creative process.

To my parents,

Your unwavering support and boundless love have provided the foundation upon which I stand. You have instilled in me the values of hard work, resilience, and the beauty of simplicity. This collection is as much yours as it is mine.

To my siblings,

You have been my first friends and lifelong companions. Your laughter, kindness, and shared memories are woven into the fabric of these poems.

To my friends,

Thank you for being my sounding board, my critics, and my cheerleaders. Your insights, whether gentle or tough, have helped shape my work into what it is today.

CHAPTER ONE

The Illusion of Expertise

"Guru" Culture: When Everyone's an Expert

It seems like everywhere you look these days, there's a self-proclaimed "guru" waiting to offer advice—about your finances, your relationships, your mental health, your career, even how you should feel on a random Tuesday. We live in an age where social media influencers, YouTube personalities, and even those with a flashy website can gain a massive following overnight, simply because they say the right things in the right tone. But here's the problem: popularity doesn't equal wisdom.

Why Popularity Doesn't Equal Wisdom

In the world of social media, what gets rewarded isn't always what's accurate. Often, it's what's *entertaining*. The catchy one-liners, the dramatic stories, the motivational speeches—they sound good and they *feel* good, but they might not always *be* good for you. The advice that goes viral is often the simplest, the easiest to digest. "Follow your passion." "Just believe in yourself." "Cut out negativity." But real life is messy and complicated, far too complex to be solved by a single motivational quote.

Popularity is a poor measure of expertise. Just because someone has millions of followers doesn't mean they understand your unique circumstances, your struggles, or your goals. They don't know your backstory or the challenges you're facing. And yet, their advice can feel so compelling that we take it as gospel, forgetting that a big follower count doesn't automatically make someone right.

The Echo Chamber of Bad Advice

The online world is full of echo chambers—places where the same ideas and advice get repeated over and over again until they become "truth." You hear the same phrases, the same life hacks, the same "proven methods" repeated by different influencers, and it creates this illusion that if *everyone* is saying it, it must be true. But that's not always the case.

Think about how many times you've heard things like, "You need to hustle 24/7 if you want to succeed" or "The early bird gets the worm." It's not that these statements don't hold any truth; it's that they're not universal truths. They might work for some people, but they might be terrible advice for others. The echo chamber makes you feel like you're the odd one out if you don't agree or if a certain piece of advice doesn't resonate with you. But reality is far more nuanced than that.

Spotting Red Flags in 'Expert' Guidance

So, how do you know when you're being fed bad advice by a so-called expert? There are a few red flags to watch out for. One of the biggest is *overconfidence*. If someone claims to have all the answers, be wary. True experts understand that the world is full of gray areas. They admit when they don't know something, and they're open to being wrong.

Another red flag is the promise of "quick fixes." Life is rarely that simple. Anyone who tells you that you can solve all your problems with a single course, a single strategy, or a single mindset shift is probably overselling. Real progress takes time, effort, and a willingness to adapt. It's messy, it's uncertain, and it definitely doesn't fit into a neatly packaged 5-step formula.

Lastly, beware of advice that dismisses your instincts or tries to make you feel like you're doing something wrong for questioning it. The best advice empowers you; it doesn't make you feel small or stupid.

Advice Overload: Too Much Noise, Too Little Sense

We are drowning in advice. It comes from our social media feeds, podcasts, friends, family, and even random articles we stumble upon online. The sheer volume of advice available can be overwhelming, and often, it's contradictory. One expert says you need to wake up at 5 AM to succeed, while another says night owls are more productive. One influencer tells you to cut out all carbs, while another swears that balance is key. And in this sea of opinions, it's hard to know what to believe and what to ignore.

How to Filter Out the Clutter

Filtering through this barrage of advice is a skill in itself. One of the first steps is learning to trust your gut. Not every piece of advice is meant for you, and that's okay. It's essential to understand your own strengths, weaknesses, and goals before you start applying advice willy-nilly.

Ask yourself, "Does this make sense for *my* situation?" Instead of asking, "Is this advice good?" a more helpful question is, "Is this advice good *for me*?" Because even good advice can turn out to be bad advice if it doesn't align with your reality. Think of yourself as the editor of your life, sifting through the noise and deciding what gets published in your own story.

The Dangers of Overanalyzing Advice

But there's a trap here too—overanalyzing advice. When you're so focused on finding the "right" way, you can end up paralyzing yourself with endless research and analysis. You'll find yourself constantly second-guessing every decision, wondering if maybe, just maybe, that one influencer's routine or that article's method would have been better for you. And before you know it, you're so stuck in weighing your options that you never actually take action.

Remember, there's no perfect advice that guarantees success. It's about trial and error, about testing what works for you. It's okay to make mistakes along the way; they're part of the learning process. And sometimes, moving forward with imperfect action is better than standing still, waiting for the perfect solution.

Quality vs. Quantity: Less is Often More

The truth is, we don't need more advice. We need *better* advice, the kind that actually takes our unique circumstances into account. Most of the time, sticking to one or two principles that genuinely resonate with you is more effective than trying to follow ten different methods at once. It's about depth, not breadth.

Think of advice like a toolbox. You don't need 50 different tools to fix a problem; you need the *right* tool for the job. And sometimes, you don't even need a tool—you just need to trust yourself to figure things out. The best advice isn't a one-size-fits-all solution; it's a guide that helps you understand how to create your own solutions.

Mistakes of the Majority: Why Conventional Wisdom Fails

Conventional wisdom has a lot of appeal. After all, if the majority of people believe something, it must be true, right? But the problem with following the crowd is that crowds can be wrong. In fact, history is full of examples where the majority got it totally backward—whether it's the belief that the earth was flat or that margarine was healthier than butter. Just because everyone believes something doesn't mean it's correct.

Herd Mentality: Blindly Following the Crowd

Herd mentality can be comforting. When you're part of the majority, you feel a sense of safety, like you're making the "right" decision simply because so many others are making the same one. But following the crowd can also lead to stagnation. It can make you resistant to new ideas, even when those ideas could be the key to your growth.

Think about it: how many times have you stuck with a job you didn't like because everyone told you it was the "responsible" thing to do? Or how often have you followed a career path, a diet plan, or even a relationship model just because it was what people around you expected? Herd mentality can keep you from taking risks, from exploring your true potential, and from finding what genuinely makes you happy.

The Trap of "It Worked for Me" Stories

One of the most common forms of advice is the classic "it worked for me" story. These stories can be inspiring, but they're not always applicable to everyone. Just because someone made a million dollars using a particular strategy doesn't mean that strategy will work for you. They had their own set of circumstances, their own skills, and their own timing, which all contributed to their success.

What we don't see in these stories are the hidden factors—the privileges, the connections, the lucky breaks that played a role. It's not that these people are lying; it's just that they're only showing us a small part of the picture. And when we try to copy-paste their story into our own lives, we often end up frustrated, wondering why it didn't work out the same way for us.

Understanding Different Contexts and Realities

Every piece of advice exists within a context, and no two contexts are exactly alike. What works for someone living in a big city with a strong support network might not work for someone living in a small town trying to make it on their own. What's effective for a 20-year-old fresh out of college might be irrelevant for someone in their 40s with a family to support.

Recognizing this is liberating. It allows you to let go of the pressure to follow advice that doesn't align with your reality. Instead of feeling like you're failing when someone else's strategy doesn't work for you, you can focus on understanding your own circumstances. You can adapt, tweak, and make adjustments that suit *your* life, rather than trying to fit your life into someone else's framework.

The Perils of Surface-Level Thinking

We live in a world where everyone's in a hurry. We want instant gratification, instant solutions, and instant understanding. But here's the catch: most advice is geared towards surface-level thinking. It deals with symptoms rather than causes. It tells you *what* to do, but rarely delves into the *why* behind it. This approach creates a big gap between knowing and truly understanding.

Band-Aid Solutions: Fixing the Symptoms, Ignoring the Root

Have you ever followed advice that seemed to make things better for a while, only to find yourself right back where you started after a few weeks or months? This is the curse of band-aid solutions. It's like taking painkillers for a broken leg. Sure, the pain might go away temporarily, but without proper treatment, that leg isn't going to heal.

Think about financial advice, for instance. A lot of popular advice focuses on cutting back on small luxuries—skipping your daily coffee or cutting down on eating out. But rarely do these tips address deeper issues, like underemployment, systemic barriers, or a lack of financial literacy in the education system. It's easier to tell someone to give up their $5 latte than to confront the larger problem of income inequality or stagnant wages. But is it really helpful? Probably not.

The same goes for relationships. You'll often hear simple, catchy advice like "Just communicate better" or "Never go to bed angry." But relationships are complex, layered with years of individual experiences, personality traits, and unresolved emotional baggage. A quick fix might help you get through one argument, but it won't teach you how to understand each other deeply or navigate the difficult phases of a long-term relationship.

Superficial Motivation: Why It Fades

Motivation is a classic area where advice falls into the trap of surface-level thinking. How many times have you watched a motivational video, felt fired up, and thought, "Yes, this time I'll stick to my goals!"—only for that fire to fizzle out in a few days? It's not that there's anything wrong with motivational videos or speeches; they can be a great spark. But without a deeper understanding of what truly drives you, that spark won't ignite a lasting flame.

Why does this happen? Because most motivation advice doesn't dig into the underlying reasons behind why you struggle to stay consistent. Maybe it's a lack of a structured plan. Maybe it's unaddressed fears or limiting beliefs. Or perhaps it's simply the wrong goal for you, chosen because it sounds good, not because it's aligned with your values.

Real, lasting motivation doesn't come from a video clip or a quote. It comes from clarity—clarity about what you want, why you want it, and how you're going to achieve it. And that clarity often requires asking yourself tough questions, reflecting on your past experiences, and being brutally honest about what's holding you back.

Digging Deeper: The Role of Self-Reflection

One of the most underrated tools for evaluating advice is self-reflection. Yet, it's something that rarely gets emphasized in the noise of self-help content. Reflecting on your own experiences, successes, and failures can give you more insight than any outside advice. It helps you see patterns in what has worked for you and what hasn't, allowing you to understand which advice fits into your life and which doesn't.

Imagine you've tried following productivity hacks like waking up at 5 AM because that's what all the top performers claim to do. But every time you've tried, you find yourself feeling tired and irritable, and your productivity actually suffers. Instead of forcing yourself to follow the advice because "successful people do it," self-reflection allows you to recognize that maybe your natural rhythm is different. Maybe you're more of a night owl, and your most productive hours are late at night. This insight is far more valuable than any one-size-fits-all advice you'll come across online.

Self-reflection is about being your own coach, asking yourself what you need at this moment, what's holding you back, and how you can move forward in a way that feels right for *you*. It's not always easy—it requires patience and a willingness to face uncomfortable truths—but it's the key to separating the advice that will help you from the advice that will hinder you.

The Myth of Universal Truths

One of the biggest myths that perpetuate bad advice is the idea that certain truths apply universally. Whether it's the "best morning routine" or the "right way to network," these so-called universal truths are often based on selective stories and anecdotal evidence. Yet, the self-help industry thrives on selling these oversimplified ideas because they offer a sense of certainty in a world that is inherently uncertain.

Success Stories: The Hidden Variables

The success stories that we hear so often—of people who quit their jobs, started a business, and became millionaires—often leave out crucial details. They don't tell you about the financial cushion they had, the connections that helped them get started, or the specific market conditions that made their business thrive. Instead, they present their success as a direct result of following a particular formula, encouraging you to follow the same path.

But here's the thing: success is rarely linear. It's not just about what someone *did*; it's about the circumstances they did it in, the timing, the resources available to them, and even a bit of luck. When you strip away these variables, you end up with advice that sounds nice but doesn't hold up when you try to apply it to your life.

This isn't to say that you can't learn from others' experiences. You absolutely can. But it's important to approach these stories with a critical eye, understanding that what worked for them might not work for you. Success leaves clues, but those clues need to be adapted, not copied.

"Follow Your Passion" and Other Clichés

Few pieces of advice are more popular—and potentially more misleading—than "follow your passion." It's the kind of advice that gets shared in graduation speeches and motivational seminars, often with the implication that if you just pursue what you love, the money, success, and fulfillment will naturally follow. But reality is far more complicated.

Following your passion can work beautifully—if you have the right support systems, market demand, and skills to turn that passion into a sustainable career. But for many, it's not that simple. What happens if your passion isn't profitable? What if you have responsibilities that require a stable income? What if you don't even know what your passion is yet? These are the questions that "follow your passion" advice often ignores.

A more nuanced version of this advice would be: "Follow your passion *thoughtfully*." It's about finding the balance between what you love, what you're good at, and what the world needs. It's about understanding that sometimes, you need to do what's necessary now so you can pursue your passion later. It's not as catchy as a three-word slogan, but it's far more practical.

Why "One Size Fits All" Rarely Fits Anyone

Most advice is designed to appeal to the masses. It aims to be as broadly applicable as possible, and in doing so, it loses the depth and nuance needed to address individual needs. It's like a clothing brand that only makes shirts in one size. Sure, it might fit some people perfectly, but for many, it will be too loose or too tight.

The problem with "one size fits all" advice is that it ignores context. It doesn't take into account your strengths, your weaknesses, your past experiences, or your future goals. It assumes that everyone is starting from the same place and heading towards the same destination, when in reality, everyone's path is different.

What's far more helpful is advice that acknowledges its own limitations. Advice that says, "Here's what worked for me, but it might not work for you—and that's okay." Advice that encourages you to take what resonates and leave the rest, rather than trying to mold yourself into someone else's vision of success.

The Comfort Trap: Why We Gravitate Toward Simplistic Advice

When life gets complicated, simplistic advice is like a warm blanket. It gives us something to cling to, a way to make sense of the chaos. But the comfort it provides is often an illusion. It feels safe, but it can be dangerously misleading. It encourages us to overlook the complexities, to settle for easy answers rather than wrestling with the difficult questions.

Why the Brain Loves Easy Solutions

Our brains are wired for efficiency, constantly seeking shortcuts to conserve energy. This is known as cognitive ease—a preference for the familiar, the straightforward, and the simple. It's why we're drawn to advice that promises clear solutions to complex problems, like "Think positive and good things will happen" or "Just work hard, and success will follow." These phrases are easy to digest, but they often come with blind spots.

Take the advice "Think positive." On the surface, it seems harmless, even helpful. After all, maintaining a positive outlook can be beneficial. But when positivity becomes a blanket solution, it can turn toxic. It can lead people to ignore legitimate challenges, dismiss their own negative emotions, and push aside the need for deeper healing or change. It turns a nuanced emotional process into a catch-all mantra, making it seem like positivity is a magic bullet for all of life's struggles.

The reality is that some of the most important work we do in life happens when we confront discomfort—when we face our fears, process our losses, and acknowledge our limitations. Real growth isn't always cheerful or uplifting. Sometimes, it's gritty and painful, but it's also necessary. Simplistic advice encourages us to skip over these crucial steps, offering short-term comfort at the expense of long-term understanding.

The Illusion of Control: Why We Seek Certainty

Another reason we cling to simplistic advice is that it gives us a sense of control. Life is unpredictable, and that unpredictability can be scary. We don't like the idea that some things are beyond our influence, that no matter how many steps we follow or how many rules we adhere to, there will always be an element of chance. So, we look for advice that suggests otherwise—advice that promises a formula, a method, a way to guarantee success.

Think about the countless "10-Step" guides and "Ultimate Roadmaps" that flood self-help sections and social media feeds. They imply that if you just follow these steps, you'll achieve a certain outcome. But life isn't a linear path; it's more like a winding road with unexpected turns and detours. A guide might help you navigate some of those turns, but it can't account for everything. It can't predict the challenges that are unique to your journey, the opportunities that will come your way, or the obstacles you'll need to overcome.

This illusion of control is particularly prevalent in advice around success and productivity. We're told that if we adopt the right habits, wake up at the right time, and organize our schedules perfectly, we'll inevitably become successful. But what this advice often overlooks is the role of external factors—things like economic conditions, access to resources, support networks, and even luck. It's easier to believe that success is entirely within our control than to accept that sometimes, no matter how hard we try, the outcome is out of our hands.

The Problem with Binary Thinking

Another trap that oversimplified advice falls into is binary thinking—seeing things in black and white, as either good or bad, right or wrong. This kind of thinking reduces complex issues into a choice between two extremes. For example, "You're either a leader or a follower," "You're either rich or you're poor," or "You're either a winner or a loser." These kinds of statements are catchy, but they're also deeply flawed.

Life is full of shades of gray, of middle grounds, of situations that don't fit neatly into either/or categories. Binary thinking encourages us to ignore those nuances, to overlook the messy in-between spaces where real life actually happens. It tells us that if you don't fit into one category, you must belong to the other, even though that's rarely the case.

For instance, in the world of entrepreneurship, you might hear that you either have a "fixed mindset" or a "growth mindset," as if those are the only two options. But in reality, most people have a mix of both, depending on the context and situation. Someone might have a growth mindset when it comes to learning a new skill but struggle with a fixed mindset when dealing with personal setbacks. Recognizing this complexity allows for more self-compassion and understanding, rather than labeling yourself as simply one or the other.

The Emotional Appeal of Advice: When Feelings Trump Facts

One of the reasons certain types of advice spread like wildfire is because they appeal to our emotions. They make us feel seen, understood, validated. And while there's nothing wrong with wanting to feel those things, it's important to recognize when emotional appeal is being used to mask a lack of substance.

Advice That Confirms Our Biases

One of the most common forms of emotionally appealing advice is the kind that confirms our existing beliefs. It tells us what we already want to hear, reinforcing our worldview rather than challenging it. This is known as confirmation bias, and it's one of the biggest obstacles to personal growth. It feels good to be told that we're right, but growth often comes from being willing to admit when we're wrong.

For example, if you're naturally an introvert, you might be drawn to advice that says "Introverts make the best leaders" or "Quiet people have deeper insights." While there may be truth to these statements, they can also keep you from acknowledging the ways in which your introversion might hold you back, like difficulty networking or reluctance to speak up in group settings. It's not about labeling introversion as good or bad; it's about being open to advice that challenges your assumptions and pushes you to grow beyond your comfort zone.

The Seduction of Victim Mentality

Another emotionally charged piece of advice often revolves around embracing a victim mentality. It's the kind of advice that encourages you to blame external circumstances for your struggles—your boss, your upbringing, the economy, or even society at large. While it's true that external factors can play a significant role in our lives, focusing solely on these can keep you stuck in a cycle of helplessness.

This kind of advice appeals to our desire to avoid responsibility, to say, "It's not my fault, it's out of my control." And while it's important to acknowledge the challenges we face, it's equally important to recognize where we do have power and agency. The best advice acknowledges both—your struggles and your strengths, your obstacles and your opportunities. It empowers you to take action even when the odds aren't in your favor, rather than simply accepting the role of a passive observer in your own life.

Why We Love a Good Success Story

Stories are powerful, and few stories are as compelling as those of transformation. We love hearing about the person who was down on their luck, tried a new approach, and turned everything around. It's why so many pieces of advice are packaged with anecdotes—stories of how someone went from zero to hero, from broke to billionaire, from struggling artist to global sensation.

But as inspiring as these stories can be, they often leave out the crucial context that made that success possible. They don't tell you about the years of struggle that preceded the turning point, or the mentors and connections that played a crucial role, or even the sheer randomness that might have tipped the scales. Instead, they focus on the moment when everything changed, making it seem like following the same path will lead to the same results.

It's easy to get swept up in the emotion of these stories, to think, "If they did it, I can too." And in many ways, that mindset can be motivating. But it's also important to recognize the difference between inspiration and instruction. A story can inspire you to take action, but it shouldn't be mistaken for a step-by-step guide to achieving the same results. Everyone's path is different, and your journey won't look exactly like anyone else's.

The Danger of Overgeneralization

Overgeneralization is another common flaw in much of the advice we hear. It's when advice is given as if it applies to everyone, everywhere, in every situation. But life is not one-size-fits-all, and advice that ignores the specific context is bound to miss the mark.

When Advice Ignores Cultural and Social Context

One area where overgeneralization becomes particularly problematic is when advice crosses cultural boundaries. Advice that works in one society or culture may be irrelevant, or even harmful, in another. For example, in some cultures, aggressive self-promotion is seen as a sign of confidence and ambition, while in others, it may be viewed as arrogance or a lack of humility.

Yet, many self-help books and motivational speakers promote a single way of doing things—usually based on Western, individualistic values—without considering how those methods might be received in other contexts. They forget that what works in Silicon Valley might not work in a small town in rural India, or that a method that succeeds in New York City might fail in a conservative community elsewhere. Good advice acknowledges these nuances, recognizing that the same approach won't yield the same results for everyone.

Oversimplification of Success: "Just Do It" and Other Myths

"Just do it." "Hustle harder." "If you want it badly enough, you'll make it happen." These phrases have become mantras in the world of personal development, but they're deeply flawed because they oversimplify the complex nature of human motivation and success.

The idea that you can will your way to success if you just work hard enough ignores the many factors that can get in the way—mental health struggles, financial limitations, systemic inequalities, and plain old burnout. It's easy to tell someone to keep pushing, but sometimes, what they really need is permission to rest, to reflect, or to take a different path altogether.

The Path Forward: Developing a Discernment for Advice

After wading through the noise of simplistic solutions, the allure of expertise, and the appeal of emotionally charged guidance, it becomes clear that the problem isn't just about bad advice—it's about how we engage with advice in the first place. The solution isn't to shut out all guidance but to develop a sense of discernment. This means learning to recognize which advice is genuinely useful and which is just noise.

Cultivating Self-Awareness

At the heart of this discernment is self-awareness. Understanding yourself—your values, your goals, your unique challenges—acts like a filter. It allows you to distinguish advice that aligns with your journey from advice that may steer you off course. It's about knowing when to lean into the guidance of others and when to trust your own instincts.

Self-awareness helps you realize that the person giving you advice may not fully understand your circumstances. They might be speaking from a position of privilege or experience that is vastly different from your own. This doesn't make their advice useless, but it does mean that you need to adapt it to your reality, taking the parts that resonate and leaving the rest behind.

The Art of Asking the Right Questions

One of the most effective ways to break through the illusion of expertise and the trap of oversimplification is by asking the right questions. When you receive advice, don't just ask, "Does this sound good?" Instead, ask deeper questions like:

- *Does this advice apply to my specific situation?*

- *What assumptions is this advice based on? Are they true for me?*
- *If I follow this advice, what might I be overlooking?*
- *Who is benefiting from this advice being popularized?*

These questions help you shift from being a passive receiver of advice to an active evaluator. They empower you to weigh the merits and limitations of what you hear, turning advice into a tool rather than a prescription. This process may feel more time-consuming and uncertain than simply following instructions, but it's a necessary step toward finding advice that truly serves you.

Embracing Ambiguity and Trusting Your Journey

Most importantly, recognizing that not all advice is meant for you is a way of embracing the ambiguity of life. It's about letting go of the pressure to find the one right answer or the perfect path. This ambiguity can be uncomfortable because it requires you to take risks, make mistakes, and accept that some of the outcomes will be beyond your control.

But embracing this ambiguity also means embracing freedom—the freedom to carve out your own path, to experiment, to adjust as you go. It's about finding the courage to sit with uncertainty and trusting that you'll find your way, even without a roadmap.

In doing so, you come to realize that the most valuable advice is often the one that encourages you to listen to yourself more closely. It's the kind that respects your ability to learn from experience, that doesn't try to mold you into someone else's version of success. It's the advice that supports you as you become more of who you already are, rather than urging you to become something you're not.

A Final Thought: It's Not About Rejecting Advice, But Redefining It

In the end, the goal isn't to reject all advice—it's to redefine your relationship with it. Recognize advice as a tool, not a script. See it as something that can inspire and guide, but not dictate. Remember that behind every piece of guidance is a human being with their own biases, their own successes and failures, their own stories. Their advice may come from a place of good intentions, but it's up to you to decide how it fits into the story you're writing for yourself.

Because the truth is, no one else is living your life. No one else has walked in your shoes or faced your challenges in quite the same way. And while advice can illuminate the path ahead, only you can decide where to step next.

And that's the most empowering realization of all: that the real wisdom lies not in the advice itself but in your ability to shape it, adapt it, and ultimately, trust your own voice amidst the noise.

CHAPTER TWO

When Common Sense Isn't So Common

Common sense—advice that seems obvious and self-evident—is supposed to be a guiding light, a fallback when more complex guidance isn't available. Yet, the problem with common sense is that it's not always as universally applicable as it seems. What's considered "common sense" can be shaped by cultural norms, social media trends, and even popular self-help clichés that sound great but don't always stand up to scrutiny. One of the most frequently cited yet misleading pieces of advice is to "just follow your passion." But is it really that simple?

"Just Follow Your Passion" and Other Misleading Myths

Why Passion Alone Won't Pay the Bills

"Follow your passion," they say. The phrase is plastered across motivational posters, quoted in viral tweets, and recited by well-meaning mentors. But the truth is, passion alone isn't a business plan. It won't guarantee a steady income, nor will it magically make the hurdles disappear. It's not that passion isn't important—having a genuine interest in your work can be a powerful driver. It can help you push through challenges, and make your work feel less like a chore. But to treat passion as the *only* necessary ingredient is to ignore the more practical realities of life: bills, rent, and financial responsibilities don't care how passionate you are. They care whether or not you can pay.

Many people who have been convinced by the "just follow your passion" mantra find themselves disillusioned when their dream doesn't translate into a paycheck. Imagine a talented photographer who loves capturing moments but struggles to find clients. Or a musician pouring their heart into compositions but facing a sea of competition. In these cases, passion might be the fuel, but without a strategy, it's just that—fuel without a vehicle.

When Chasing Dreams Becomes a Nightmare

Sometimes, the chase for passion can turn into an obsession, one that blinds you to the sacrifices you're making. You pour everything into your dream—time, money, energy—and suddenly, you realize that you've put yourself in a financially precarious situation. You might find yourself struggling to balance the pursuit of your passion with the practicalities of everyday life. The dream becomes a source of stress rather than fulfillment.

This isn't to say that you should abandon your passion, but rather, it's important to be realistic about what it takes to turn that passion into something sustainable. This might mean taking a job you're not crazy about to support your passion on the side, or learning skills that complement your dream, like marketing or business management, to make it more viable. It's about knowing that passion needs to be balanced with pragmatism.

Building Skills vs. Following Emotions

A common mistake many make is thinking that passion should lead, and everything else will follow. But what if we flipped that script? What if, instead of asking, "What am I passionate about?" you asked, "What am I good at?" or "What skills can I develop that align with my interests?" Building skills can often be a more reliable path to long-term success than simply following a passion. Skills can be honed, adapted, and applied across different fields, offering flexibility that a singular passion might not.

The reality is that many successful people don't start out by doing what they love. They start out by doing what they can do well. Over time, as their skills grow and they gain confidence, they begin to find aspects of their work that they can become passionate about. This is the balance that often gets lost in the romanticized narrative of "just follow your passion." Sometimes, the path to loving your work is not straight, but rather a winding journey of developing your strengths and discovering new interests along the way.

The Problem with "Quick Fixes"

Why Overnight Success Stories are Mostly Fiction

Another piece of common advice that sounds like common sense but often misleads is the idea of the "overnight success." Whether it's a tech entrepreneur who becomes a billionaire before turning 30 or an influencer who gains millions of followers in months, the allure of rapid success is strong. Social media feeds us a constant diet of these stories, making us feel like we're just one brilliant idea away from instant fame or fortune. But for every overnight success story you hear, there are hundreds of untold stories about years of struggle, failure, and small wins that eventually add up.

What you don't see behind the curtain are the countless late nights, the rejections, the anxiety of wondering if things will ever work out. We're often shown the highlight reel but not the behind-the-scenes grind. And so, we start to believe that if success doesn't come quickly, we must be doing something wrong. We internalize the idea that struggling is a sign of failure, rather than a natural part of the process.

Real Change Takes Time: Patience is Underrated

There's a reason the phrase "good things take time" has endured. Real, lasting success is often a slow burn, not a flash in the pan. Think about a tree growing—it's not glamorous or rapid, but with time, it becomes something strong and enduring. The same is true for building a career, a business, or any meaningful endeavor. It's about showing up consistently, even when it feels like nothing is happening, even when the progress is imperceptible. Patience isn't just a virtue; it's a necessity when it comes to navigating the reality of long-term growth.

Yet, in a culture that prizes speed—fast results, quick profits, instant gratification—patience often feels like a luxury. It's easy to lose sight of the fact that the people we admire for their achievements often spent years or even decades working in obscurity before anyone noticed their brilliance. Their "overnight" success was years in the making, built on the back of perseverance and quiet determination.

Learning to Trust the Process

Trusting the process means understanding that progress is often uneven. It means accepting that there will be times when you feel stuck, or when it seems like you're moving backward. But just like a plane that temporarily dips before gaining altitude, these moments are often part of a larger trajectory toward growth. Learning to trust the process doesn't mean abandoning your goals—it means being patient with the time it takes to get there and being kind to yourself in the process.

It's about recognizing that setbacks are not failures but lessons in disguise. Each obstacle is a chance to adjust your approach, to gain insight, and to come back stronger. This mindset shift is what separates those who give up when things get tough from those who keep going and eventually break through.

Advice That Feels Good But Hurts Later

Short-term Wins vs. Long-term Losses

There's also the problem of advice that feels good in the moment but comes with hidden costs down the road. Take, for example, the idea of "always say yes to opportunities." It sounds positive and proactive, but if you follow this advice without discernment, you can quickly find yourself overwhelmed, stretched too thin, and unable to focus on what truly matters. Saying yes to everything means you may end up with a calendar full of obligations that don't align with your long-term goals.

The same applies to feel-good mantras like "you're perfect just the way you are." While it's important to accept yourself, this can sometimes become an excuse to avoid growth or to resist challenging your own behaviors. True self-acceptance doesn't mean complacency—it means understanding your strengths and weaknesses and working on yourself from a place of love, not guilt or pressure.

How Feel-Good Mantras Can Mislead You

Many popular sayings, like "live in the moment" or "trust your gut," sound wise but are often misinterpreted. Living in the moment is valuable, but it doesn't mean neglecting to plan for the future. Trusting your gut is important, but it shouldn't replace thoughtful analysis, especially in complex situations where emotions can cloud judgment.

Feel-good advice is comforting because it appeals to our desire for simplicity. It gives us a sense of control, a sense that we can make everything okay with the right mindset. But the reality is that life is more nuanced. It requires us to balance positivity with realism, hope with pragmatism.

Facing the Truth Even When It's Uncomfortable

The most powerful advice is often the least comfortable. It's the advice that challenges us to look in the mirror and acknowledge where we need to change, where we need to let go, and where we need to push harder. It's the advice that doesn't shy away from the complexity of life but rather, embraces it fully. It's about finding the courage to face reality, even when it's not what you want to hear. Because while feel-good advice may offer a momentary boost, only truth will guide you through the difficult times.

As we peel back the layers of conventional wisdom, we begin to see the cracks in many popular pieces of advice. It's easy to get swept up in ideas that sound like common sense, but a closer look often reveals how oversimplified they are. Life is rarely as straightforward as a slogan, and those who thrive in the long run are the ones who recognize this complexity.

Short-Term Wins vs. Long-Term Losses (Continued)

The Temptation of Quick Gratification

One of the biggest traps in following advice that prioritizes short-term wins is that it aligns with our brain's natural inclination for instant gratification. We want to see results, and we want them *now*. Whether it's starting a new fitness routine, launching a side hustle, or building a relationship, the desire for immediate rewards can cloud our judgment. It's easy to be lured by promises of fast progress, but these often come with strings attached. For instance, fad diets that promise rapid weight loss might seem effective at first, but they can be unsustainable and even harmful in the long run. Similarly, get-rich-quick schemes rarely deliver the lasting success they advertise, and more often than not, they lead to disappointment.

This is where many people stumble: they focus on what's easy today without considering the cost tomorrow. It's like a runner sprinting at the start of a marathon, only to collapse before the finish line. True progress is made when we're willing to pace ourselves, to endure the discomfort of delayed gratification, and to focus on the bigger picture. It means accepting that the most meaningful achievements often take time to materialize. This perspective is not as glamorous as the promise of a "hack" or a shortcut, but it's a more reliable path to long-term fulfillment.

Sustainable Growth Over Flashy Results

Another issue with prioritizing short-term wins is that it can cause you to focus on tactics rather than strategy. Tactics might give you a quick boost—like running a flashy marketing campaign that grabs attention or launching a product with a lot of hype—but if you don't have a solid foundation, those gains won't last. It's like building a house with a beautiful exterior but a shaky foundation: it might look impressive initially, but it won't withstand the storms.

Sustainable growth, on the other hand, is built on steady progress, consistent effort, and a willingness to make sacrifices today for a better tomorrow. It's about thinking beyond the immediate future and asking yourself, "What will this decision look like in five years?" or "How does this align with my long-term vision?" It's about planting seeds and being patient enough to let them grow. This is why the advice of "slow and steady wins the race" may seem old-fashioned, but it holds more wisdom than many of the flashy mantras of our time.

How Feel-Good Mantras Can Mislead You (Continued)

The Rise of Social Media Gurus and Oversimplified Wisdom

In the age of social media, advice often comes in bite-sized, shareable quotes—snippets that are easy to consume but rarely provide the depth needed to address complex issues. We've all seen those perfectly curated posts that tell us to "stay positive" or "follow your heart." They sound good, they feel good, and they get likes and shares. But in reality, these simplified messages can do more harm than good when taken at face value.

Take the popular mantra "stay positive." Positivity is important, no doubt, but toxic positivity—the idea that you should always look on the bright side and ignore negative feelings—can invalidate genuine struggles and prevent you from addressing real challenges. It can make you feel guilty for experiencing anxiety, sadness, or frustration, as if acknowledging these emotions means you're failing. But in reality, it's normal and even healthy to experience a full range of emotions. Pretending that everything is fine when it's not only pushes those feelings deeper, making them harder to deal with in the long run.

True resilience comes from facing challenges head-on, acknowledging the difficulty, and finding a way through. It's about knowing that it's okay to have bad days, to feel discouraged, and to take time to process those feelings. Positivity has its place, but so does realism.

How One-Size-Fits-All Advice Fails Us

Another issue with feel-good advice is that it often ignores the diversity of individual experiences. It treats everyone as if they are starting from the same point, facing the same challenges, and moving toward the same goals. But life is far more varied than that. What works for one person might not work for another, and advice that sounds great in one context might be completely out of place in another.

For example, the advice to "take risks and follow your dreams" might be inspiring for someone with a financial safety net, but for someone living paycheck to paycheck, that same advice can be reckless. The message to "quit your 9-to-5 and become your own boss" might sound empowering, but it overlooks the reality that entrepreneurship is not for everyone and that stability is a privilege, not a given. There's a reason why people are drawn to simple, feel-good advice—it provides comfort and reassurance. But real wisdom lies in understanding that every path is unique, and what matters is finding what works best for *you*, not for some idealized version of yourself.

Facing the Truth Even When It's Uncomfortable (Continued)

Why Brutal Honesty is the Best Gift You Can Give Yourself

The hardest advice to accept is often the advice that forces us to confront our own shortcomings. It's much easier to believe that the problem lies outside of us—that our circumstances, other people, or plain bad luck are to blame. But sometimes, the real barrier is our own mindset or behavior. Being willing to look in the mirror and ask, "What am I doing wrong?" is one of the most courageous things you can do. It's a process of shedding illusions and facing reality, even when it hurts.

Maybe you've been procrastinating on a goal and blaming it on a lack of time, but deep down, you know it's fear holding you back. Maybe you've been telling yourself that you're waiting for the "right moment" to start something new, but in reality, you're just scared of failing. The ability to be brutally honest with yourself can be a turning point. It allows you to break out of self-imposed limitations and make real changes.

Discomfort as a Catalyst for Growth

Discomfort is often seen as something to avoid, but in many cases, it's the key to growth. Think about it—most significant transformations happen outside of your comfort zone. Whether it's pushing through the awkwardness of learning a new skill, having difficult conversations that lead to better relationships, or taking a leap into unfamiliar territory, discomfort is the bridge between where you are and where you want to be.

Yet, much of the advice we hear is about avoiding discomfort. It tells us to take the easy route, to seek out what feels good, and to avoid anything that causes stress or anxiety. But if you want to achieve something meaningful, you need to get comfortable with being uncomfortable. It's about learning to see discomfort not as a threat, but as a sign that you're stretching yourself beyond your limits and growing into something new.

The Value of Asking the Tough Questions

Facing the truth also means being willing to ask yourself tough questions—questions that don't have easy answers. "Am I really happy with where I am?" "Am I avoiding something difficult because it scares me?" "What do I need to change to become the person I want to be?" These questions are uncomfortable because they force us to confront the gap between our current reality and our ideal self. But they are also necessary for real, lasting change.

Most people avoid these questions because they fear what the answers might reveal. But those who dare to ask them often find clarity, direction, and a sense of purpose that they never had before. It's about being willing to dig deep, to challenge your assumptions, and to understand that sometimes, the best advice is the one that doesn't sugarcoat reality.

As we dig further into the complexities behind common advice, it becomes clear that many of the messages we absorb every day are just the surface level of much deeper ideas. The simplicity of these messages often disguises their shortcomings, and as we peel away these layers, we find a richer, more nuanced understanding of what it takes to truly navigate life's challenges.

Advice That Feels Good But Hurts Later (Continued)

When Motivation Becomes a Mirage

The rise of motivational content in today's culture has its place. Sometimes, a well-timed pep talk or a video filled with inspiring music can give you that extra boost you need. But there's a downside to constantly relying on motivational advice. It can create a kind of dependency, where you feel like you need that next hit of positivity to keep going. Motivation becomes like sugar—it gives you a quick rush, but the energy it provides is often short-lived.

It's easy to feel inspired after watching a video or reading a quote that tells you to "never give up" or that "you are enough." But what happens when the high wears off? What happens when you're left alone with your thoughts, facing the grind of everyday life? That's when reality hits, and it can feel like a sudden drop. If all you have is a collection of feel-good quotes but no actionable strategy, it's like standing on a stage with no script—you might look confident for a moment, but the act can only last so long.

True, sustainable progress doesn't come from relying on bursts of motivation. It comes from cultivating discipline and habits that keep you moving forward, even on days when you don't feel particularly inspired. It's about recognizing that not every moment is going to be filled with excitement and that sometimes, the most important work is done when nobody is watching, and the world is silent.

The Trap of Focusing on Feelings Over Facts

Another common issue with feel-good advice is that it often places too much emphasis on how you *feel* rather than what is *true*. There's this idea that if something feels right, it must be right. But feelings can be deceptive. They can be influenced by fear, insecurity, and social conditioning. For example, you might feel like you're not good enough for a particular opportunity, but that doesn't mean you aren't. It just means that your feelings are lying to you, shaped by past experiences and self-doubt.

On the flip side, you might feel confident in a decision that isn't actually the best choice, simply because it aligns with what you want to believe. This is where the phrase "trust your gut" can be misleading. Gut instincts are valuable, but they aren't infallible. Sometimes, trusting your gut can lead you straight into a situation you should have avoided, like trusting a charismatic but unreliable business partner or diving into a market without doing your research because you just "feel" it will work out.

True wisdom comes from balancing emotions with facts, from recognizing the power of your feelings while still keeping a firm grasp on reality. It's about being able to step back from your emotions and ask, "Is this how I feel, or is this actually true?" It's a tough balance to strike, but those who master it find themselves making more grounded and effective decisions.

How Feel-Good Mantras Can Mislead You (Continued)

The Pressure to Always Be Positive

In a world where positivity is often pushed as the ultimate solution, there's an unspoken pressure to maintain a cheerful demeanor, even when life is falling apart. Social media especially has amplified this, with endless posts about gratitude, happiness, and "choosing joy" no matter the circumstances. But what happens when you're not feeling joyful? What happens when life hits you with challenges that no amount of positive thinking can erase?

The truth is, forcing yourself to be positive all the time can actually be detrimental. It can make you feel like there's something wrong with you for experiencing negative emotions, even though those feelings are a natural part of being human. The reality is, it's okay to have bad days, to feel frustrated, sad, or even angry. These emotions are part of the human experience, and they can teach us valuable lessons about ourselves and the world around us.

By always striving to maintain a positive outlook, you might miss out on the insights that come from facing your struggles head-on. You might miss the chance to process your emotions fully, to understand why you're feeling a certain way, and to make changes that actually address the root of the issue. It's about finding a balance—appreciating the power of positivity while also giving yourself permission to acknowledge when things aren't okay.

When Being Real Is Better Than Being Positive

Imagine a friend who's always telling you to "look on the bright side" whenever you're going through a tough time. While their intentions might be good, it can feel invalidating, as if your struggles aren't worth acknowledging. Now, think about the difference when you have a friend who's willing to sit with you in your discomfort, who listens to your frustrations without trying to fix them, and who reminds you that it's okay to feel the way you do. This kind of support can be far more comforting than relentless optimism because it's grounded in reality.

Being real, being authentic, and being willing to confront the messiness of life can create a deeper connection with others and with yourself. It's about embracing the full spectrum of human experience and recognizing that true growth comes from navigating both the highs and the lows. It's about understanding that life isn't always about smiling through the pain, but sometimes about acknowledging the pain and learning to move forward, scars and all.

Facing the Truth Even When It's Uncomfortable (Continued)

Why Avoiding Hard Realities Sets You Up for Failure
One of the toughest truths to accept is that avoiding hard realities doesn't make them go away. In fact, it often makes them worse. It's like ignoring a leaky roof because you don't want to deal with the hassle of fixing it—eventually, that small leak turns into a flood, and you're left with far more damage than if you had addressed it early on.

This is true in every aspect of life, from personal relationships to career choices. Ignoring a problem at work because it's uncomfortable to address can lead to bigger issues down the road, like missed promotions or job dissatisfaction. Overlooking red flags in a relationship might keep things smooth for a while, but eventually, those unresolved issues will come to the surface.

The discomfort of facing these realities is temporary, but the consequences of avoiding them can be lasting. It's about choosing short-term discomfort for long-term peace, about having those difficult conversations, and about taking the time to really understand what's going wrong before it spirals out of control. It's about being willing to admit when you don't have it all together and reaching out for help when you need it, instead of pretending that everything is fine.

The Power of Vulnerability in Embracing Your Flaws
It's ironic, but the moment you stop trying to be perfect is often the moment you become more powerful. Vulnerability is not a weakness; it's a strength. It's the ability to show up as you are, without the need for masks or pretenses. It's the courage to say, "I don't have all the answers," or "I'm struggling right now," and to be okay with that.

This kind of honesty can be liberating. It frees you from the pressure of constantly trying to meet unrealistic standards and allows you to focus on what really matters—growth, learning, and progress. It creates space for deeper connections, as people can relate to you on a human level, rather than seeing you as an unapproachable figure of success. And it allows you to accept yourself, flaws and all, as a work in progress.

Why Facing the Truth is the Ultimate Form of Self-Respect

At the end of the day, facing the truth is about respecting yourself enough to be honest with yourself. It's about saying, "I deserve to know the reality of my situation, even if it's not what I want to hear." It's about taking ownership of your choices and understanding that while you can't control everything, you can control how you respond to what life throws your way.

There's a certain dignity in refusing to accept easy answers and instead demanding the deeper truths, even when they're uncomfortable. It's this commitment to truth—both the bitter and the sweet—that ultimately leads to a more grounded and resilient approach to life. It's not easy, but then again, most things that are truly worth having rarely are.

As we bring this chapter to a close, it's essential to reflect on the journey we've taken through the pitfalls of commonly accepted advice. The phrases and mantras that saturate our culture often present an oversimplified view of life, masking the complexity and richness of human experience. We've examined how the allure of passion, the mirage of motivation, and the pressure to maintain an unwaveringly positive outlook can lead us astray, and we've seen how the value of authenticity and truth can pave the way for genuine growth and understanding.

Redefining Success on Your Own Terms

In a world obsessed with quick fixes and overnight successes, it's crucial to redefine what success means to you. It's not about conforming to societal standards or following the well-trodden paths that others have laid out before you. Instead, it's about recognizing your unique journey, the skills you're building, and the values you hold dear. Success is not a one-size-fits-all template; it's a personal narrative, shaped by your choices and experiences.

Embracing the Journey, Not Just the Destination

Life is a journey filled with twists and turns, peaks and valleys. Instead of fixating solely on the end goals, we must learn to appreciate the process—the moments of struggle, learning, and growth. These experiences, however uncomfortable, are the very fabric of our lives. They teach us resilience, adaptability, and the profound strength that comes from overcoming challenges.

As you navigate your own path, remember to honor your feelings while also grounding yourself in reality. Seek advice that encourages critical thinking rather than blind acceptance. Surround yourself with individuals who challenge you to think deeply and question the status quo. Authentic connections are built on vulnerability and shared experiences, fostering a supportive environment where growth can flourish.

CHAPTER THREE

Unpacking the Psychology Behind Bad Advice

Advice is often delivered with the best of intentions, but understanding the psychological underpinnings behind why we follow it can help us navigate the complexities of decision-making. Cognitive biases—those mental shortcuts that our brains take—play a pivotal role in shaping our beliefs and influencing our choices. This chapter delves into these invisible forces, shedding light on how they can lead us astray.

Cognitive Biases: The Invisible Forces Shaping Our Beliefs

Our minds are not objective processors of information; rather, they are influenced by various cognitive biases that can distort our perception of reality. By unpacking these biases, we can gain insight into why certain pieces of advice resonate with us, even when they may not be grounded in reality.

The Confirmation Bias Trap: Seeking What You Want to Hear

One of the most pervasive biases is confirmation bias, which leads us to seek out information that confirms our existing beliefs while dismissing contrary evidence. This tendency can result in a dangerous cycle, where we become trapped in our own echo chambers. For instance, if someone believes that a particular diet is the only way to lose weight, they may ignore scientific research supporting other methods and focus solely on success stories that align with their viewpoint.

This bias is particularly dangerous when it comes to advice, as it can lead to a narrow-minded approach to life. When you're only seeking validation for your choices rather than evaluating the merits of different perspectives, you risk making uninformed decisions that could have serious consequences. It's essential to actively challenge this bias by exposing yourself to diverse viewpoints, engaging in critical thinking, and questioning your assumptions.

Anchoring: When One Idea Dominates Your Thinking

Another cognitive bias that can distort our judgment is anchoring, which occurs when we rely too heavily on the first piece of information we receive. This initial data point serves as a reference point that shapes our subsequent thoughts and decisions. For example, if someone is presented with a high initial price for a product, they may perceive any subsequent discounts as more valuable than they truly are, even if the final price is still inflated.

In the realm of advice, anchoring can manifest when we fixate on one popular piece of guidance or a single success story. This singular focus can overshadow alternative options and critical analysis. When faced with a decision, it's crucial to gather a wide range of information before making conclusions, ensuring that your thoughts are not dominated by a single perspective.

Availability Heuristic: Why Recent Events Skew Reality

The availability heuristic is another cognitive shortcut that leads us to judge the likelihood of an event based on how easily we can recall similar instances. This bias can skew our perception of reality, particularly when recent events are fresh in our minds. For example, after hearing about a few viral success stories from social media influencers, one might assume that anyone can achieve fame through similar means, disregarding the hard work, luck, and timing involved.

This heuristic also affects how we interpret advice. When popular advice trends circulate, they can create a perception of validity based solely on their visibility rather than their merit. It's vital to dig deeper and consider the broader context before adopting any piece of advice that seems appealing because it's currently trending.

Emotional Persuasion: When Advice Plays with Your Feelings

Emotions can heavily influence our decision-making, often leading us to make choices that we might later regret. Advice that appeals to our emotions can be particularly manipulative, and understanding the tactics behind this emotional persuasion can empower us to make better choices.

Manipulation Tactics in Popular Advice

Certain types of advice rely on manipulation tactics that exploit our emotional vulnerabilities. This is especially prevalent in self-help culture, where success stories are often presented in a way that evokes strong feelings of hope, fear, or inadequacy. Advertisements and influencers may showcase idealized versions of success that can be misleading, leading individuals to chase unattainable goals based on an emotional reaction rather than a rational assessment.

How Fear and Hope Are Used Against Us

Fear and hope are potent emotional drivers that can be weaponized in advice-giving. Marketers frequently tap into these emotions to sell products or services by suggesting that failure to act could lead to dire consequences. For example, a weight-loss program might emphasize the fear of health risks associated with obesity, using emotionally charged messaging to compel individuals to enroll.

Conversely, hope can create a false sense of security. When we latch onto advice that promises quick results or miraculous transformations, we may become overly optimistic about our chances of success, neglecting the realities of hard work and dedication required for meaningful change.

Understanding Emotional Triggers

Recognizing our emotional triggers can help us approach advice more critically. We must ask ourselves why a particular piece of guidance resonates with us. Is it tapping into our fears? Offering false hope? By becoming aware of these triggers, we can approach advice with a healthier skepticism, ensuring that our decisions are rooted in rational thought rather than emotional manipulation.

The Power of Storytelling: Good Stories, Bad Lessons

Stories are a powerful medium for sharing advice, but they can be a double-edged sword. Anecdotes can captivate us, but they can also lead us astray if we don't critically evaluate their applicability to our own lives.

When Anecdotes Become Dangerous Advice

While personal stories can provide valuable insights and inspiration, they often fail to account for individual differences and complexities. A success story about someone who achieved wealth overnight may overlook the years of hard work, setbacks, and unique circumstances that paved the way for that success. When we rely too heavily on anecdotes, we risk generalizing experiences that may not be relevant or attainable for us.

Separating Facts from Narratives

To navigate this challenge, it's important to cultivate discernment. Instead of taking stories at face value, we should seek to understand the underlying factors that contributed to the outcomes presented. What were the individual's skills, resources, and contexts? Were there lessons to learn, or merely outcomes to admire? By dissecting stories and separating facts from narratives, we can glean valuable lessons without falling victim to misleading advice.

How to Read Between the Lines of a Story

Finally, learning to read between the lines of a story can equip us to sift through the noise and identify the core lessons applicable to our lives. Ask yourself critical questions: What assumptions are being made? Are there biases at play? What might be left unsaid? This analytical approach can help you extract meaningful insights while avoiding the pitfalls of blindly following anecdotal advice.

The Role of Social Influence on Decision-Making

The decisions we make, including the advice we choose to follow, are heavily influenced by those around us. Social dynamics play a significant role in shaping our beliefs and behaviors. This section examines how social influence can lead us to accept questionable advice.

The Bandwagon Effect: Joining the Crowd

The bandwagon effect is a cognitive bias that leads individuals to adopt certain behaviors, follow trends, or purchase items primarily because others are doing so. This phenomenon can be particularly powerful in the context of advice. When a particular piece of guidance gains popularity—whether it's a new health trend, a financial strategy, or a lifestyle change—many feel compelled to hop on the bandwagon without critically evaluating its merits.

This effect is exacerbated by social media, where the visibility of certain ideas can create a false sense of validity. For instance, if numerous influencers are promoting a specific diet or workout regimen, their followers may feel pressured to conform, believing that if everyone else is doing it, it must be right. However, this can lead to misguided decisions based on popularity rather than personal relevance or effectiveness.

Peer Pressure and Its Impact on Choices

Peer pressure is another powerful force influencing our decision-making process. We often look to our friends, family, and colleagues for guidance, and the desire to fit in can lead us to accept advice that may not be in our best interest. For example, if your friends are all investing in a certain stock or pursuing a particular lifestyle, you might feel compelled to follow suit, even if it doesn't align with your values or financial goals.

Understanding the role of peer pressure in shaping our choices is vital for developing a more critical approach to advice. It's important to ask yourself whether your desire to follow the crowd is based on sound reasoning or merely the need for social acceptance. By fostering a strong sense of self and prioritizing your values, you can resist the pull of peer pressure and make decisions that truly resonate with you.

The Impact of Authority on Advice Acceptance

We often turn to authority figures for guidance, believing that their expertise can lead us to better decisions. However, this deference to authority can also lead to uncritical acceptance of advice that may not be suitable for our individual circumstances.

The Authority Bias: Trusting Experts Blindly

The authority bias is the tendency to attribute greater accuracy to the opinion of an authority figure, regardless of their actual expertise in a specific area. While it's beneficial to seek advice from knowledgeable individuals, the risk lies in assuming that their expertise translates universally to your situation. For example, a successful entrepreneur's advice on building a startup may not apply to someone in a completely different industry or with different resources.

To combat this bias, it's essential to evaluate the qualifications and context of those offering advice. Just because someone has achieved success doesn't mean their journey or strategies will work for you. By critically analyzing the relevance of the advice based on your unique circumstances, you can make more informed choices.

The Dangers of Blindly Following Authority

The dangers of following authority figures without question can be seen in various historical contexts. From corporate scandals to misguided medical practices, the consequences of blind obedience can be severe. When individuals fail to question authority, they may unknowingly participate in harmful practices or support flawed systems.

It's crucial to remember that authority figures are human too. They can make mistakes, hold biases, or promote outdated methods. Always approach advice from authority with a healthy degree of skepticism. Ask yourself: What evidence supports their claims? Are they considering diverse perspectives? What biases might they have?

Self-Reflection: The Key to Making Better Choices

While it's easy to get swept up in external influences and biases, self-reflection serves as a powerful tool for breaking free from the chains of bad advice. By taking time to examine your beliefs and values, you can develop a clearer understanding of what truly matters to you.

Understanding Your Values and Goals

Before acting on advice, spend time reflecting on your personal values and long-term goals. What is important to you? What do you hope to achieve? Understanding your priorities can provide a solid foundation for evaluating any guidance you receive.

For instance, if your core value is sustainability, advice to invest in a particular company may not align with your beliefs if that company is known for harmful practices. By aligning your decisions with your values, you create a more meaningful and authentic path forward.

Questioning the Source of Your Advice

When presented with advice, take a moment to consider its source. Who is providing this guidance? What are their motives? Are they trying to sell you something, or do they genuinely have your best interests at heart? By critically evaluating the source of advice, you can discern whether it is worth considering or if it should be dismissed.

Cultivating an Open Mind while Maintaining Skepticism

Self-reflection also involves cultivating an open mind while maintaining a healthy skepticism. Be willing to explore new ideas and perspectives, but do so with a critical eye. Ask probing questions, seek evidence, and weigh different viewpoints. This balanced approach allows you to expand your understanding while safeguarding against potentially harmful advice.

The Importance of Context in Advice

One of the most critical aspects of evaluating advice is recognizing the importance of context. What works for one person in a specific situation may not be applicable to you in a different context. This is particularly relevant in areas like career advice, financial guidance, or personal relationships.

Recognizing Individual Differences

Every individual is unique, with different experiences, resources, and circumstances. Advice that may seem sound for one person could be entirely inappropriate for another. For instance, a strategy that worked for a startup founder in Silicon Valley might not be relevant for an entrepreneur in a small town with limited resources.

Before accepting advice, consider your individual differences and the specifics of your situation. Are there factors that make the advice less applicable to you? By acknowledging these nuances, you can avoid the trap of one-size-fits-all thinking.

The Role of Timing in Advice Validity

Timing also plays a crucial role in the validity of advice. The relevance of certain guidance may change based on evolving circumstances, trends, or societal shifts. For example, financial advice that was valid during a booming economy may not apply during a recession. Similarly, career guidance may vary based on industry developments and technological advancements.

Staying informed about changes in your field and being open to reassessing advice based on new information will ensure that your decisions are based on the most relevant and current understanding available.

The Influence of Emotional States on Decision-Making

Our emotional states play a critical role in how we process information and make decisions, including the advice we choose to follow. Understanding the relationship between emotions and decision-making can illuminate why we sometimes accept advice that isn't in our best interest.

How Emotions Cloud Judgment

When we are in a heightened emotional state—be it happiness, fear, anxiety, or anger—our judgment can become clouded. Research shows that individuals often make impulsive decisions when experiencing strong emotions. This phenomenon can lead to accepting advice that resonates with our current feelings rather than critically evaluating its validity.

For example, if you're feeling anxious about your career, you might be drawn to advice promising quick results or radical changes, even if such guidance lacks a solid foundation. In these moments, it's crucial to recognize the influence of your emotional state and pause before making decisions based solely on feelings.

Emotional Reactions to Advice: The Power of Relatability

When advice is presented in a relatable way, it can trigger emotional reactions that skew our perception of its value. This is often seen in the realm of motivational speaking, where speakers share personal stories that resonate deeply with audiences. While these narratives can be inspiring, they can also lead to the acceptance of flawed advice.

Consider a speaker who recounts a story of their rapid success after taking a particular risk. The relatability of their journey may evoke strong emotions, compelling listeners to adopt similar strategies without thoroughly considering the risks involved or the specifics of their own situation.

Strategies for Managing Emotional Responses

To avoid being swayed by emotions when evaluating advice, practice emotional regulation techniques. These can include mindfulness meditation, deep breathing exercises, or simply taking a moment to reflect before reacting. By creating space between your emotions and your decision-making process, you can approach advice with a clearer, more rational mindset.

The Role of Narrative in Advice Acceptance

Narratives shape our understanding of the world, often influencing how we interpret advice. The power of storytelling is a double-edged sword; while it can convey valuable lessons, it can also lead to the acceptance of misleading or oversimplified advice.

The Persuasiveness of Anecdotal Evidence

Anecdotal evidence is often more persuasive than statistical data because it appeals to our emotions and personal experiences. When someone shares their success story tied to a specific piece of advice, it can create a powerful connection that makes it hard to question the advice's validity.

However, anecdotal evidence is not a substitute for rigorous analysis. Just because one person's experience was positive does not mean that the same outcome will apply to you. Acknowledging the limitations of anecdotal evidence is essential for making sound decisions.

Discerning Between Good Stories and Bad Lessons

As you encounter narratives, consider the underlying lessons being conveyed. Are they universal, or do they hinge on specific circumstances? Understanding the context behind a story allows you to extract meaningful insights without blindly accepting the advice tied to it.

For example, a story about a person who achieved great wealth through risky investments may highlight qualities like courage and decisiveness. However, it's crucial to recognize that the same strategy may not be suitable for everyone. Extract the valuable traits without adopting the potentially harmful behavior.

Cultivating Critical Thinking Skills

The ability to think critically is essential for navigating the vast landscape of advice. By honing your critical thinking skills, you can better analyze the advice you receive and determine its relevance to your situation.

Questioning Assumptions

A key component of critical thinking is the willingness to question assumptions. When presented with advice, ask yourself what underlying beliefs inform it. Are these beliefs rooted in evidence, or are they based on outdated or biased perspectives?

For instance, advice to pursue a traditional career path might stem from societal norms that prioritize stability over personal fulfillment. By questioning these assumptions, you can decide whether the advice aligns with your values and aspirations.

Engaging in Constructive Skepticism

Constructive skepticism involves questioning the validity of advice while remaining open to new ideas. Rather than dismissing advice outright, seek evidence and context to support it. This approach encourages healthy discourse and allows you to engage with diverse perspectives.

When faced with advice, ask questions like:

- What evidence supports this claim?
- Are there alternative viewpoints to consider?
- How does this advice apply to my specific circumstances?

Engaging in this dialogue with yourself can enhance your ability to discern valuable advice from misleading guidance.

The Impact of Digital Media on Advice Reception

In today's digital age, the way we consume information has changed dramatically. The internet, social media, and various platforms have made it easier to access a wealth of advice, but this accessibility also comes with challenges.

The Misinformation Epidemic

Misinformation can spread rapidly online, leading individuals to accept advice that is not grounded in reality. Social media platforms often amplify sensationalized content that grabs attention, regardless of its accuracy. This phenomenon is particularly prevalent in health, finance, and personal development sectors.

To navigate this landscape, cultivate digital literacy. Assess the credibility of sources before accepting advice. Look for qualifications, evidence, and diverse viewpoints. Reliable information often comes from experts who provide nuanced insights rather than simplistic solutions.

The Illusion of Connection

Social media creates an illusion of connection, leading individuals to feel more inclined to trust advice from strangers. This can be dangerous, as you may find yourself following guidance from individuals whose motivations and expertise are unclear.

Remember that online personas are curated representations of individuals. Just because someone presents themselves as an authority online does not mean they possess the knowledge or experience to back it up. Approach online advice with caution, and prioritize guidance from credible, well-established sources.

Building a Personal Framework for Evaluating Advice

To navigate the complexities of advice effectively, it's helpful to develop a personal framework for evaluating it. This framework can serve as a guiding compass, helping you sift through advice and make informed decisions.

Identifying Core Values

Begin by identifying your core values and what is most important to you. This could include aspects such as integrity, creativity, personal growth, or financial stability. Knowing your values allows you to evaluate advice based on whether it aligns with your priorities.

For example, if personal growth is a core value, you may prioritize advice that encourages stepping out of your comfort zone, even if it feels risky.

Establishing a Decision-Making Process

Create a structured process for evaluating advice. This could involve several steps:

1. **Initial Assessment**: Consider your initial feelings toward the advice. Does it resonate with you? Why or why not?
2. **Contextual Analysis**: Analyze the context of the advice. Is it relevant to your current situation? Are there specific factors to consider?
3. **Source Evaluation**: Research the source of the advice. What qualifications do they have? Are they transparent about their motives?
4. **Alternative Perspectives**: Seek out alternative viewpoints. What do other experts or individuals say about this advice? Are there counterarguments to consider?
5. **Personal Reflection**: Take time to reflect on how the advice aligns with your values and long-term goals.

By implementing this framework, you can cultivate a more disciplined approach to decision-making, enabling you to make choices rooted in authenticity rather than blind acceptance.

As we conclude this chapter, it's crucial to recognize the intricate interplay between our psychology and the advice we encounter in our daily lives. The influences of cognitive biases, emotional states, and social dynamics can obscure our judgment, leading us to accept guidance that may not serve our best interests.

We've uncovered how **cognitive biases**, such as confirmation bias and the availability heuristic, can distort our perception of reality. These invisible forces shape our beliefs and decisions, often pushing us toward advice that aligns with what we already believe rather than challenging us to grow. By becoming aware of these biases, we can cultivate a more critical mindset, allowing us to sift through the noise of popular advice.

The **emotional undercurrents** that accompany decision-making cannot be understated. Our feelings profoundly affect how we interpret advice, often leading us to make impulsive choices based on transient emotions. As we've discussed, taking a moment to pause and reflect on our emotional states can help us navigate this complex landscape more effectively. Practicing emotional regulation techniques will empower us to approach advice with clarity and intention, rather than reactiveness.

Moreover, the **power of storytelling** and the influence of narratives remind us of the need to discern between valuable lessons and potentially harmful guidance. While stories can inspire and educate, they can also oversimplify complex issues, leading us to draw conclusions that do not consider our unique contexts. By developing the skill to evaluate the relevance of anecdotes, we can extract wisdom without succumbing to the allure of sensationalized narratives.

In today's digital age, where misinformation spreads rapidly, cultivating **digital literacy** becomes imperative. Understanding how to evaluate sources critically and distinguish between credible information and unfounded claims will serve as essential tools in our decision-making arsenal. By remaining vigilant about the quality of the advice we consume, we can guard ourselves against the pitfalls of bad guidance.

Lastly, the importance of establishing a **personal framework for evaluating advice** cannot be overstated. By grounding our decisions in our core values and following a structured evaluation process, we can navigate the complex world of advice with confidence and integrity. This framework will help us align our actions with our true selves, enabling us to make informed choices that resonate with our long-term goals.

In summary, the journey through the psychology of advice reveals that while guidance can be valuable, it is essential to approach it with discernment and critical thought. As we move forward in this book, let us carry these insights into the next chapters, striving to empower ourselves with knowledge and strategies that enhance our decision-making capabilities.

Together, we will continue to unravel the myths and misconceptions that surround advice, paving the way for a more informed and intentional approach to personal and professional growth. The goal is not to become mere followers of advice but to become discerning individuals who create our paths guided by wisdom, experience, and self-awareness.

CHAPTER FOUR
Breaking Free from Bad Advice

How to Develop a Critical Thinking Mindset

In a world overflowing with advice, the ability to critically evaluate guidance is essential. **Chapter 4** delves into breaking free from the constraints of conventional wisdom, empowering you to cultivate a critical thinking mindset. This chapter is your guide to navigating the sea of opinions and finding what truly resonates with your unique journey.

Asking the Right Questions Before Accepting Advice

The foundation of critical thinking lies in **questioning**. When presented with advice, it's vital to ask yourself: *Who is giving this advice? What are their motives?* Often, advice comes from a place of experience, but experiences are subjective and vary widely. Recognizing the biases of the advice-giver is crucial in assessing the validity of their guidance.

Start by considering the **context** in which the advice is offered. For example, advice on career choices may come from someone with a completely different professional background. It's essential to dissect whether their insights apply to your specific situation or if they merely reflect their circumstances. By asking questions, you gain clarity and begin to filter through the advice, determining what truly aligns with your values and goals.

Learning to Challenge Even the Experts

It's easy to assume that experts hold all the answers, but the reality is more complex. While experts often provide valuable insights based on extensive experience, their perspectives are not infallible. **Learning**

to challenge even the experts encourages you to think independently and not accept advice at face value.

When considering expert advice, examine the *evidence* that supports their claims. Are their conclusions based on recent research or anecdotal experiences? Engaging with multiple sources allows you to construct a more rounded view, giving you the confidence to question established norms and carve your own path.

For instance, in fields like health and wellness, trends can rapidly change as new studies emerge. Instead of blindly following advice from well-known figures, take the time to research and understand the science behind their recommendations. By doing so, you empower yourself to make informed decisions rather than becoming a passive recipient of information.

Building Your Own Framework for Decision-Making

Creating a personal **framework for decision-making** is essential for developing a critical mindset. This framework acts as a roadmap, guiding you through the complexities of advice and ensuring your decisions align with your core values.

Begin by identifying your **goals** and what you want to achieve. This clarity will inform your decision-making process and help you determine which pieces of advice resonate with your objectives. As you encounter advice, consider how it fits within your framework. Does it lead you closer to your goals, or does it distract you from your path?

Additionally, integrate self-reflection into your framework. After making decisions based on advice, take the time to evaluate the outcomes. Did the advice serve you well? What can you learn from the experience? This reflective practice not only enhances your decision-making skills but also fosters personal growth, allowing you to adapt your framework as needed.

Trusting Your Experience Over Someone Else's Words

Your journey is unique, and trusting your **experience** is crucial in breaking free from bad advice. While external guidance can be helpful, your insights and feelings should take precedence. Often, the advice that resonates most with you is rooted in your lived experiences.

Listen to your **inner voice**—it has valuable insights that deserve attention. By cultivating self-awareness, you can discern when advice feels right or when it contradicts your intuition. Trusting yourself doesn't mean dismissing all external guidance; rather, it means integrating it with your personal understanding to create a well-rounded perspective.

Embrace the idea that failures and setbacks are not signs of defeat but rather invaluable lessons. Reflecting on your past experiences helps you build resilience and a more profound understanding of what works for you. Each failure provides insights that can inform future decisions, allowing you to approach new advice with a nuanced perspective.

Learning from Failures: The Best Teacher You'll Ever Have

Failure often carries a stigma, but it's essential to recognize it as one of the most powerful teachers you'll encounter. Each setback offers insights that can guide your future decisions, enabling you to sift through advice more effectively.

For example, if you tried a popular productivity method and it didn't work for you, instead of discarding the entire concept of productivity advice, analyze what aspects didn't align with your style. Was it the approach, the tools used, or perhaps the time management techniques? By dissecting your experiences, you create a personalized repository of knowledge that informs your future decisions.

Moreover, sharing your experiences with others can provide valuable insights. Engaging in conversations about failures fosters a community of learning, where people can collectively dissect advice and discover what resonates with various contexts. This collaboration enriches your understanding and strengthens your critical thinking skills.

Creating Your Own Path: What Works for You

Breaking free from bad advice means recognizing that the journey is uniquely yours. There's no one-size-fits-all solution, and what works for one person may not suit another. Embrace the process of **customizing advice** to fit your reality.

To do this, begin by conducting a **self-assessment**. Understand your strengths, weaknesses, and preferences. What motivates you? What obstacles do you face? By acknowledging these factors, you can sift through advice and extract elements that resonate with your circumstances.

Experimentation is vital in this process. Don't be afraid to try different approaches and adapt them as needed. Perhaps you've read about time management techniques that worked for others but felt uncomfortable in practice. Instead of discarding the concept altogether, modify it to align with your workflow. Find a rhythm that feels natural to you, integrating aspects of various approaches until you create a method that fits seamlessly into your life.

Customizing Advice to Fit Your Reality

As you break free from bad advice, **customizing guidance** to fit your reality becomes essential. It's not enough to accept advice blindly; the real magic happens when you tailor it to your unique context.

Understanding your **strengths and weaknesses** allows you to approach advice critically. For instance, if you're an introvert seeking networking strategies, a one-size-fits-all approach may leave you feeling drained. Instead, adapt networking techniques to align with your comfort level. This customization fosters an authentic connection, enhancing your experience while minimizing discomfort.

Furthermore, understand that the effectiveness of advice can evolve over time. What worked for you in the past may no longer suit your current circumstances. As you grow and change, continually reassess the guidance you receive, ensuring it aligns with your present reality. This iterative process strengthens your ability to discern valuable advice from the noise.

Understanding Your Strengths and Weaknesses

Understanding your strengths and weaknesses is a cornerstone of developing a critical thinking mindset. By recognizing your abilities, you can confidently evaluate advice that plays to your strengths while avoiding paths that may lead to frustration.

For example, if you excel at creative thinking but struggle with analytical tasks, seek advice that encourages your creative instincts. This self-awareness allows you to filter advice through the lens of your capabilities, ensuring that you're not drawn into methods that contradict your natural inclinations.

Embrace the concept of **growth**. Acknowledge your weaknesses as areas for development rather than limitations. By seeking advice that challenges you to grow, you create opportunities for personal improvement. Emphasizing growth fosters resilience, encouraging you to embrace challenges as stepping stones toward your goals.

The Art of Experimenting and Adapting

Finally, the journey of breaking free from bad advice hinges on the **art of experimenting and adapting**. In a world filled with varying opinions, don't shy away from trial and error. Embrace experimentation as a means of discovery.

Start small. If you encounter a piece of advice that intrigues you, test it out in your life. Observe the outcomes and reflect on how it aligns with your values and objectives. If it proves beneficial, consider integrating it into your routine. If it falls flat, analyze why it didn't resonate and adjust your approach accordingly.

Adaptation is crucial in this process. As you learn from your experiments, refine your methods and approaches. This iterative cycle of experimentation allows you to navigate the complexities of advice more effectively, empowering you to develop a personalized framework that evolves with you.

How to Develop a Critical Thinking Mindset (Continued)

As we dive deeper into the elements of developing a critical thinking mindset, it's essential to recognize that this journey is not merely about rejecting bad advice but rather about cultivating an active approach to decision-making. In this section, we will explore additional strategies to empower your critical thinking, ensuring that you become adept at filtering the guidance you receive.

Building a Diverse Knowledge Base

One of the most effective ways to fortify your critical thinking is by **building a diverse knowledge base**. The more varied your experiences and knowledge, the better equipped you are to analyze advice from multiple angles. This diversity enriches your understanding and provides a broader context within which to evaluate suggestions.

1. **Read Widely**: Delve into books, articles, and research across various fields. By engaging with a variety of subjects, you expand your mental toolkit, allowing you to draw connections between seemingly unrelated concepts. For

instance, reading about psychology, economics, and philosophy can help you understand the complexities of human behavior and decision-making, informing your ability to discern valuable advice.
2. **Engage in Discussions**: Seek out conversations with people from different backgrounds and perspectives. Diverse viewpoints challenge your thinking and expose you to alternative ideas that may reshape your understanding of certain advice. Embrace constructive debates and discussions, as they encourage you to defend your beliefs and critically evaluate opposing viewpoints.
3. **Attend Workshops and Seminars**: Participating in workshops and seminars offers opportunities to learn from experts in various fields. Engage with content that challenges your existing beliefs and fosters critical thinking. These events often present real-world scenarios and case studies, allowing you to practice applying your analytical skills to practical situations.

Practicing Mindfulness in Decision-Making

Incorporating **mindfulness** into your decision-making process can enhance your critical thinking. Mindfulness encourages you to pause, reflect, and fully consider the implications of advice before acting on it. Here are some techniques to cultivate mindfulness in your decision-making:

1. **Pause Before Reacting**: When you receive advice, take a moment to pause and breathe. This pause allows you to gather your thoughts and consider the advice's relevance to your situation. Instead of reacting impulsively, use this time to evaluate the potential outcomes of following the advice.

2. **Reflect on Your Values**: Aligning advice with your core values is crucial for informed decision-making. Ask yourself how the advice aligns with your beliefs and aspirations. If it feels misaligned, it may not be worth pursuing, regardless of its popularity.
3. **Visualize Outcomes**: Take time to visualize the potential consequences of following the advice. Picture the short-term and long-term effects on your life, goals, and relationships. This mental exercise helps you assess whether the advice serves your best interests.
4. **Journal Your Thoughts**: Keep a journal to document your thoughts and feelings about the advice you receive. Writing helps clarify your emotions and thoughts, enabling you to dissect advice more objectively. Over time, reviewing your journal entries can reveal patterns in the advice you've accepted or rejected, aiding your growth in critical thinking.

Embracing a Growth Mindset

Cultivating a **growth mindset** is a powerful way to navigate the world of advice and enhance your critical thinking. Embracing the belief that your abilities can develop through dedication and hard work empowers you to view challenges as opportunities for learning.

1. **Welcome Feedback**: Instead of fearing criticism, welcome constructive feedback as a valuable source of insight. Understanding how others perceive your decisions can provide alternative viewpoints that strengthen your critical thinking. Approach feedback with curiosity rather than defensiveness, allowing it to inform your future choices.
2. **Celebrate Small Wins**: Recognize and celebrate the progress you make in your decision-making process. Whether you

successfully navigated a difficult choice or learned from a mistake, celebrating these wins reinforces your growth mindset. Acknowledging your achievements boosts confidence and motivates you to continue refining your critical thinking skills.
3. **Stay Curious**: Foster a sense of curiosity about the world around you. Approach life with a questioning attitude, exploring new ideas and perspectives. This curiosity encourages lifelong learning and keeps your critical thinking skills sharp, ensuring that you remain open to reevaluating advice as you gain new insights.
4. **Accept Challenges**: Don't shy away from difficult situations or complex advice. Instead, view them as opportunities to deepen your understanding. By embracing challenges, you develop resilience and enhance your ability to navigate the complexities of decision-making.

Leveraging Technology for Better Decision-Making

In today's digital age, leveraging technology can significantly enhance your critical thinking and decision-making skills. Here are ways to utilize technological tools effectively:

1. **Research Tools**: Utilize online databases, academic journals, and credible websites to research advice before accepting it. A simple Google search can lead you to reputable sources that provide evidence and context for the advice being offered.
2. **Critical Thinking Apps**: Consider using apps designed to promote critical thinking and decision-making. These tools often provide frameworks, exercises, and prompts that help you analyze advice more rigorously, fostering a structured approach to decision-making.

3. **Mind Mapping Software**: Mind mapping tools can help you visually organize your thoughts and analyze advice. By creating a visual representation of the concepts and relationships involved, you can better understand the complexities and implications of various pieces of advice.
4. **Online Courses**: Platforms offering online courses on critical thinking and decision-making provide valuable resources to enhance your skills. Engaging with structured learning can deepen your understanding and equip you with practical strategies for evaluating advice.

Finding Your Community of Thinkers

Surrounding yourself with a community of like-minded individuals who value critical thinking can bolster your journey. Engaging with others who share your desire for thoughtful analysis can inspire you to refine your decision-making skills further.

1. **Join Forums or Discussion Groups**: Seek out online forums or local discussion groups focused on critical thinking, philosophy, or personal development. Engaging in these spaces allows you to exchange ideas, challenge each other's perspectives, and cultivate a deeper understanding of complex issues.
2. **Attend Networking Events**: Participating in networking events can connect you with people who prioritize informed decision-making. Engage in conversations with those who inspire you, and build relationships that encourage growth and critical thinking.
3. **Mentorship**: Consider seeking a mentor who values critical thinking and offers guidance on navigating advice. A mentor can provide valuable insights and serve as a sounding board

for your thoughts and decisions, helping you develop your analytical skills.

The Ongoing Journey of Critical Thinking

As you embark on your journey of breaking free from bad advice, remember that developing a critical thinking mindset is an ongoing process. Embrace the fact that you will continuously encounter new perspectives and advice, and your ability to navigate these complexities will evolve.

- **Stay Flexible**: Life is unpredictable, and advice that may have once resonated with you may not hold the same weight in different contexts. Embrace flexibility in your thinking, allowing yourself to adapt and grow as you encounter new information and experiences.

- **Practice Regularly**: Like any skill, critical thinking requires practice. Regularly engage with challenging content, evaluate advice, and reflect on your decision-making processes. The more you practice, the sharper your critical thinking skills will become.

- **Acknowledge Growth**: As you cultivate your critical thinking mindset, acknowledge the growth you experience along the way. Celebrate your ability to navigate complex advice and make informed decisions, fostering confidence in your judgment.

By implementing these strategies, you'll be well on your way to developing a robust critical thinking mindset that allows you to break free from bad advice and create a path uniquely tailored to your life.

Continuing our journey into the development of a critical thinking mindset, it's essential to delve deeper into practical applications and the nuanced aspects of decision-making. This chapter serves as a toolkit for you to not only filter advice but also to apply critical thinking in various aspects of your life, ensuring that you craft decisions that resonate with your authentic self.

Engaging with Diverse Perspectives

To strengthen your critical thinking, it's crucial to engage with a wide range of perspectives. This engagement not only broadens your understanding but also helps you challenge your assumptions and refine your thinking process. Here are several ways to actively seek out diverse viewpoints:

1. **Cultivate Relationships with Different Thinkers**: Surround yourself with individuals who think differently from you. This could include friends, family members, or colleagues with varying opinions and backgrounds. Engage in meaningful conversations, and don't shy away from topics that may evoke differing opinions.

   o **Learn from Dissent**: Embrace disagreement as a powerful tool for growth. When you encounter opposing views, take the time to explore the rationale behind them. This practice sharpens your ability to evaluate advice critically and enables you to construct well-rounded opinions.

2. **Participate in Cross-Disciplinary Discussions**: Explore conversations that span various fields—science, art, technology, and philosophy. Cross-disciplinary discussions encourage innovative thinking and challenge the boundaries

of conventional wisdom. Attend events or webinars that invite speakers from diverse fields to share their insights and experiences.

3. **Explore Cultural Narratives**: Understanding different cultural perspectives can significantly enrich your critical thinking. Read literature, watch films, or consume media from different cultures to gain insight into various worldviews. This exploration can help you recognize biases in your thinking and appreciate the complexities of human experience.

4. **Travel and Experience New Environments**: If possible, travel to different regions or countries. Experiencing new cultures firsthand broadens your horizons and provides a wealth of knowledge that can inform your decision-making. Even local explorations—visiting different neighborhoods or attending cultural events—can offer valuable insights.

Employing Analytical Tools

Incorporating analytical tools into your decision-making process enhances your critical thinking and empowers you to dissect advice systematically. Here are a few effective tools you can utilize:

1. **SWOT Analysis**: This classic strategic planning technique can be applied to personal decision-making. Analyze the **Strengths**, **Weaknesses**, **Opportunities**, and **Threats** related to the advice you are considering. By conducting a SWOT analysis, you gain clarity about the potential impact of your decisions and can weigh the pros and cons more effectively.

- **Example**: If you receive advice to invest in a specific opportunity, conduct a SWOT analysis to determine its strengths (e.g., high potential returns), weaknesses (e.g., market volatility), opportunities (e.g., emerging trends), and threats (e.g., competition). This systematic approach helps you make more informed choices.

2. **Decision Matrix**: Create a decision matrix to evaluate multiple options based on predetermined criteria. List your options on one axis and the criteria on the other. Rate each option against the criteria and calculate a total score to identify the most viable choice.

- **Example**: If you're considering multiple job offers, list the job titles, salary, company culture, career growth potential, and work-life balance as criteria. Score each job on a scale of 1 to 10 for each criterion, and sum the scores to determine which offer aligns best with your priorities.

3. **Pros and Cons Lists**: While simple, creating a pros and cons list is a timeless and effective method for evaluating advice. It allows you to visualize the advantages and disadvantages of a particular course of action, helping you arrive at a more rational decision.

4. **Scenario Planning**: Consider potential future scenarios that could result from following a piece of advice. Envision the best-case, worst-case, and most likely outcomes. This practice enables you to foresee possible challenges and benefits, empowering you to make decisions that align with your goals.

Instilling a Habit of Reflection

Reflection is a powerful tool in developing a critical thinking mindset. Regularly engaging in reflective practices helps you assess your decisions and learn from your experiences.

1. **End-of-Day Reflections**: Take a few moments at the end of each day to reflect on the decisions you made. Ask yourself questions like:

   ○ What advice did I receive today, and how did I respond to it?

   ○ Did I make any decisions that felt rushed or uninformed?

   ○ What could I have done differently to approach the situation with greater critical thinking?

2. **Weekly Reviews**: Dedicate time each week to review your decisions and the advice you followed. Identify patterns in your thinking and assess whether you consistently gravitate toward certain types of advice. This practice fosters self-awareness and enables you to make adjustments for the future.

3. **Celebrate Learning Moments**: Instead of focusing solely on the outcomes of your decisions, celebrate learning moments. If you followed advice that didn't yield the desired results, reflect on what you learned from the experience. Recognizing growth in failure reinforces the idea that critical thinking is a journey, not a destination.

4. **Engage in Creative Expression**: Journaling, painting, or engaging in other forms of creative expression can help you

process your thoughts and feelings. Creativity often leads to breakthroughs in thinking, allowing you to articulate complex emotions and ideas related to the advice you receive.

Balancing Intuition and Rationality

While critical thinking is rooted in logic and analysis, it's also essential to recognize the role of intuition in decision-making. Your instincts can provide valuable insights, especially when combined with rational thought.

1. **Listen to Your Gut**: When weighing advice, pay attention to your gut feelings. Intuition often draws from your past experiences and emotional intelligence. If something feels off about a piece of advice, take the time to explore why that might be the case.
2. **Combine Intuition with Analysis**: Instead of viewing intuition and rationality as opposing forces, consider them complementary. Use your analytical skills to evaluate advice while also allowing your instincts to guide you. This balanced approach can lead to well-rounded decision-making.
3. **Practice Mindfulness Techniques**: Incorporating mindfulness practices, such as meditation or deep breathing exercises, can help you tune into your intuition. By quieting your mind, you create space for inner wisdom to emerge, allowing you to make decisions that resonate with your true self.

Creating Your Decision-Making Framework

As you refine your critical thinking skills, consider creating a personalized decision-making framework. This framework acts as a guide for evaluating advice and making choices that align with your values and goals.

1. **Define Your Core Values**: Identify the values that matter most to you. Are you focused on integrity, creativity, family, or personal growth? By clarifying your values, you create a foundation upon which to evaluate advice.
2. **Establish Criteria for Advice Evaluation**: Determine the criteria that advice must meet to be considered valid. This may include relevance to your situation, alignment with your values, and the credibility of the source. Having clear criteria helps you filter out noise and focus on what truly matters.
3. **Document Your Decision-Making Process**: Keep a record of your decision-making process, including the advice you considered, the analysis you conducted, and the outcomes. Documenting this journey allows you to identify what works and what doesn't, creating a feedback loop for continuous improvement.
4. **Share Your Framework**: Consider sharing your decision-making framework with trusted friends or family. Engaging others in the process can provide additional insights and foster accountability, helping you stay committed to your critical thinking journey.

Overcoming Fear of Making Mistakes

One significant barrier to developing a critical thinking mindset is the fear of making mistakes. This fear can lead to indecision and a reluctance to challenge popular advice. Overcoming this fear is crucial for your growth.

1. **Reframe Mistakes as Learning Opportunities**: Instead of viewing mistakes as failures, reframe them as valuable learning experiences. Every misstep provides insights that can inform future decisions. Embracing this perspective empowers you to take risks and learn from the journey.
2. **Limit Perfectionism**: Perfectionism can paralyze your decision-making process. Acknowledge that no decision will ever be perfect, and striving for perfection can lead to inaction. Instead, focus on making informed choices based on the best information available to you at the time.
3. **Seek Support**: Surround yourself with a supportive community that encourages risk-taking and experimentation. Share your fears with trusted individuals who can provide perspective and reassurance as you navigate the complexities of decision-making.
4. **Practice Self-Compassion**: Be kind to yourself during the decision-making process. Recognize that everyone makes mistakes and that you are not defined by them. Practicing self-compassion fosters resilience and empowers you to continue evolving your critical thinking skills.

The Continuous Journey of Critical Thinking

As we conclude this chapter, remember that developing a critical thinking mindset is an ongoing journey. The world will continually present new information, perspectives, and advice, and your ability to navigate these complexities will evolve as you grow.

1. **Embrace Change**: Change is a constant in life, and your

critical thinking skills will need to adapt as circumstances shift. Embrace change as an opportunity for growth, and remain open to reevaluating your perspectives.
2. **Stay Curious**: Never stop learning. The pursuit of knowledge is a lifelong endeavor. Continuously seek out new information, engage in diverse conversations, and remain inquisitive about the world around you.
3. **Cultivate Resilience**: Building a critical thinking mindset requires resilience. Challenges will arise, and not every decision will lead to success. Cultivating resilience enables you to bounce back from setbacks and continue refining your thinking.
4. **Share Your Insights**: As you develop your critical thinking skills, share your insights with others. Engaging in discussions about your journey not only reinforces your understanding but also helps others navigate their own paths toward critical thinking.

As we wrap up this chapter on breaking free from bad advice and developing a critical thinking mindset, it's essential to acknowledge that this journey is not a destination but an evolving process. Embracing critical thinking requires continuous effort, self-reflection, and a willingness to challenge both external advice and your internal beliefs.

The Path Forward: Embracing Continuous Growth

1. **Commit to Lifelong Learning**: The world is constantly changing, and so is the information we encounter daily. By committing to lifelong learning, you remain adaptable and open to new ideas, enabling you to assess advice critically and make informed decisions.

- **Action Step**: Set aside time each week for personal development—read books, take online courses, or engage in discussions that challenge your thinking.

2. **Build a Supportive Community**: Surround yourself with like-minded individuals who value critical thinking and personal growth. Engaging in discussions with this community provides a safe space for exchanging ideas, challenging assumptions, and refining your thought processes.

- **Action Step**: Join or create groups focused on critical thinking, such as book clubs or discussion forums, where you can collaboratively explore diverse perspectives.

3. **Practice Regular Self-Assessment**: Periodically assess your decision-making processes and the advice you have accepted. Reflect on what has worked, what hasn't, and how you can improve your critical thinking skills moving forward.

- **Action Step**: Establish a monthly reflection routine to evaluate your decisions, the advice you followed, and the outcomes. Use this time to adjust your framework for evaluating future advice.

4. **Encourage Open Dialogue**: Foster an environment where open dialogue is encouraged. Share your insights with others, and invite them to challenge your views. This practice not only strengthens your own understanding but also promotes a culture of critical thinking among your peers.

- **Action Step**: Initiate conversations that invite differing opinions and perspectives, ensuring that everyone feels comfortable expressing their thoughts without judgment.

5. **Integrate Mindfulness Practices**: Incorporating mindfulness into your daily routine enhances your ability to remain present and engage critically with the information you encounter. Mindfulness helps you distinguish between emotional reactions and rational responses, allowing for clearer decision-making.

- **Action Step**: Consider starting a mindfulness practice, such as meditation or journaling, to cultivate awareness and clarity in your thought processes.

Final Thoughts: Embrace Your Journey

As you continue your journey toward developing a critical thinking mindset, remember that every decision you make is an opportunity for growth. Embrace the challenges, learn from the missteps, and celebrate your successes.

Your journey is unique, shaped by your experiences, values, and aspirations. By trusting yourself, seeking diverse perspectives, and fostering a mindset of curiosity and resilience, you can confidently navigate the complexities of life, free from the constraints of bad advice.

Ultimately, breaking free from bad advice is about reclaiming your agency. It's about understanding that while advice can serve as a guide, the most authentic and effective decisions come from within. Trust your instincts, challenge the status quo, and craft a path that reflects your true self.

Key Takeaways

- **Lifelong Learning**: Commit to continuous personal development.

- **Community Engagement**: Build a supportive network for collaborative growth.

- **Self-Assessment**: Regularly evaluate your decision-making process.

- **Open Dialogue**: Encourage diverse perspectives in discussions.

- **Mindfulness**: Integrate mindfulness practices to enhance clarity and awareness.

In conclusion, embrace your power to discern what advice serves you best. With critical thinking as your ally, you can forge your path with confidence, authenticity, and purpose, navigating the complexities of life while staying true to yourself.

CHAPTER FIVE

The Art of Giving (and Receiving) Better Advice

How to Give Advice Without Becoming a Know-It-All

Giving and receiving advice is an essential part of our human experience. However, the effectiveness of this exchange can vary greatly depending on how we approach it. This chapter explores the nuances of offering and accepting advice, emphasizing the importance of empathy, humility, and self-awareness. We'll dive deep into practical strategies that allow us to become more mindful advisors while remaining open to the insights of others.

Understanding the Limits of Your Experience

One of the most common pitfalls in giving advice is assuming that your experiences are universally applicable. While your journey may have provided valuable lessons, it's crucial to recognize that others may be facing different circumstances, perspectives, and challenges.

- **Self-Reflection**: Before offering advice, take a moment to reflect on your own experiences. Ask yourself whether your insights are genuinely applicable to the situation at hand.

- **Cultural Sensitivity**: Consider the cultural and contextual differences that may shape another person's experience. What works for you may not resonate with someone from a different background or situation.

This recognition of our limitations not only fosters humility but also opens the door to a richer exchange of ideas. By acknowledging that you don't have all the answers, you create space for others to share their unique insights and experiences.

The Importance of Listening Before Speaking

Effective advice-giving begins with active listening. It's tempting to jump in with solutions before fully understanding someone's situation, but this approach often leads to misunderstandings and ineffective advice.

- **Practice Active Listening**: Make a conscious effort to listen deeply. Focus on understanding the speaker's feelings, motivations, and concerns. This means putting away distractions and giving your full attention.

- **Ask Clarifying Questions**: Before offering any advice, ask open-ended questions to ensure you grasp the nuances of the situation. Questions like "Can you tell me more about that?" or "How did that make you feel?" can lead to a deeper understanding.

Listening not only enriches your perspective but also builds trust with the person seeking your advice. They are more likely to feel heard and valued, which makes your eventual insights more impactful.

Building Empathy in Conversations

Empathy is the bridge that connects advice-givers and receivers. It allows you to step into someone else's shoes and see the world from their perspective, enriching your ability to provide meaningful guidance.

- **Practice Empathetic Communication**: Use "I" statements to express understanding. For example, "I can see how that would be challenging for you" demonstrates empathy and validates the other person's feelings.

- **Share Personal Experiences Sparingly**: While sharing your own experiences can help illustrate your points, be cautious not to overshadow the other person's narrative. Your experiences should serve as examples, not as the definitive answer.

By fostering empathy, you create a more supportive environment for meaningful dialogue. This approach can transform an ordinary conversation into a powerful exchange of insights.

Learning to Receive Advice Without Losing Yourself

While giving advice is essential, being able to receive advice gracefully is equally important. It requires vulnerability and the willingness to embrace constructive feedback without compromising your identity.

- **Embrace a Growth Mindset**: Understand that receiving advice is an opportunity for growth. Instead of viewing it as criticism, see it as a chance to learn and develop.

- **Know Your Core Values**: When receiving advice, clarify your own values and goals. This self-awareness will help you sift through advice, identifying what aligns with your vision and what doesn't.

By maintaining your sense of self while remaining open to external insights, you empower yourself to make informed decisions that resonate with your true identity.

How to Take Criticism Constructively

Constructive criticism can be a valuable tool for personal and professional development. However, the way we receive and interpret criticism can significantly impact our growth journey.

- **Avoid Immediate Reactions**: When faced with criticism, take a moment to pause before responding. This helps prevent knee-jerk reactions driven by emotion.

- **Seek Clarification**: If feedback is unclear, don't hesitate to ask for examples or clarification. This proactive approach demonstrates your willingness to learn and improves your understanding of the criticism.

Learning to view criticism as a resource rather than a setback will enable you to grow from your experiences and refine your decision-making process.

Identifying Advice That's Worth Trying

In an age where advice is abundant and easily accessible, discerning which guidance is genuinely worth your time and energy can be challenging.

- **Evaluate Credibility**: Consider the source of the advice. Is it someone with expertise in the area they're discussing? Have they demonstrated success or knowledge in that field?

- **Assess Practicality**: Before implementing advice, evaluate whether it aligns with your unique circumstances and values. What works for one person may not work for you, so be sure to customize the advice to fit your reality.

By honing your ability to filter advice, you can prioritize strategies that resonate with your journey and facilitate your growth.

Balancing Openness with Self-Confidence

Being open to new ideas while maintaining self-confidence is crucial for navigating the complex landscape of advice.

- **Cultivate a Confident Mindset**: Trust in your abilities and judgment while remaining open to external insights. This balance allows you to integrate valuable advice without compromising your sense of self.

- **Practice Assertiveness**: When discussing advice or feedback, communicate your thoughts confidently. Use assertive language that expresses your opinions and feelings without belittling others.

Striking this balance enhances your ability to engage meaningfully with both advice-giving and receiving, fostering a healthy exchange of ideas.

The Future of Advice: Learning in the Digital Age

As we navigate an increasingly digital world, the landscape of advice is evolving rapidly. The abundance of information available online presents both opportunities and challenges.

- **Navigating Information Overload**: With countless sources of advice at our fingertips, it's essential to develop critical thinking skills to assess the credibility and relevance of the information.

- **Embracing Lifelong Learning**: Utilize digital platforms for continuous learning. Online courses, webinars, and forums can provide valuable insights from diverse perspectives, enriching your understanding and broadening your horizons.

Why It's Okay to Be Wrong and Learn from It

In the realm of advice, no one has all the answers. It's natural to make mistakes and misjudge situations.

- **Reframe Mistakes as Learning Opportunities**: Instead of fearing failure, embrace it as a part of the learning process. Analyze what went wrong and how you can apply those lessons in the future.

- **Normalize Vulnerability**: Share your experiences of misjudgment and the lessons you've learned with others. This openness fosters a culture of acceptance and growth, allowing everyone to learn from one another's mistakes.

Embracing the idea that it's okay to be wrong fosters resilience and adaptability in your approach to advice.

Curating Your Personal Learning Network

Your learning network plays a crucial role in shaping the quality of advice you receive and the insights you share.

- **Diverse Perspectives**: Surround yourself with individuals from various backgrounds and experiences. This diversity enriches your understanding and exposes you to different viewpoints.

- **Engagement and Interaction**: Actively participate in discussions, whether online or in-person, to engage with your network. This interaction not only enhances your learning but also strengthens relationships.

By curating a robust personal learning network, you empower yourself to navigate the complexities of advice-giving and receiving with confidence and insight.

In our interconnected world, where communication flows freely and advice is readily available, navigating the nuances of giving and receiving counsel is more critical than ever. This chapter delves deeper into the complexities of advice exchange, aiming to equip you with the tools needed to share your insights effectively while remaining open to the wisdom of others. The art of giving and receiving advice is not merely about imparting knowledge; it's about fostering relationships built on understanding, respect, and shared growth.

Understanding the Limits of Your Experience

When offering advice, it's essential to acknowledge the limits of your own experiences. Many people fall into the trap of believing their journey is a universal template. However, this belief can lead to advice that feels dismissive or irrelevant to others.

- **Contextual Awareness**: Every person's journey is shaped by a myriad of factors, including background, culture, and personal circumstances. Recognizing this diversity is crucial in providing valuable advice. For instance, a piece of career advice that worked well for you might not be applicable to someone in a different industry or facing distinct challenges.

- **The Dunning-Kruger Effect**: This cognitive bias occurs when individuals with limited knowledge in a domain overestimate their expertise. Being aware of this tendency can help you stay humble and approach advice-giving with a healthy dose of skepticism about your own capabilities.

By understanding the limits of your experience, you not only improve the quality of the advice you provide but also create an atmosphere of mutual respect and learning.

The Importance of Listening Before Speaking

Active listening is one of the most powerful tools in effective communication. It lays the foundation for meaningful advice exchange.

- **The Power of Non-Verbal Cues**: Pay attention to the speaker's body language and tone. Sometimes, what isn't said can be just as important as the words spoken. Non-verbal cues can reveal underlying emotions or concerns that may be essential for you to consider before offering advice.

- **Refrain from Interrupting**: Allow the person to express their thoughts fully before you respond. Interruptions can make individuals feel undervalued, and it might prevent you from fully grasping their perspective.

Engaging in this way cultivates trust and encourages deeper conversations. The more you listen, the more insightful your advice will become.

Building Empathy in Conversations

Empathy is at the heart of effective communication. It allows you to connect with others on a deeper level, fostering a sense of safety and openness in the conversation.

- **Practice Reflective Listening**: After someone shares their story or problem, summarize what you've heard and reflect it back to them. This not only demonstrates that you're actively listening but also helps clarify any misunderstandings. For example, you might say, "It sounds like you're feeling overwhelmed because of X situation. Is that right?" This approach invites further dialogue and shows that you genuinely care about their feelings.

- **Avoid Judgment**: Approach every conversation without preconceived notions or judgments. Everyone's experiences are valid, and by suspending your judgment, you create a safe space for sharing.

Building empathy doesn't just enrich the advice-giving experience; it transforms it into a collaborative process where both parties can learn and grow.

Learning to Receive Advice Without Losing Yourself

The flip side of giving advice is receiving it. Often, this can feel daunting, especially if the advice challenges your current beliefs or practices.

- **Assessing Value**: Not all advice will resonate with you, and that's perfectly okay. Cultivating the ability to discern which pieces of advice align with your values and aspirations is vital. As you evaluate advice, consider the source, the context, and how it relates to your own experiences.

- **Setting Boundaries**: While it's beneficial to be open to advice, it's equally important to know your limits. If advice feels misaligned with your core values, it's perfectly acceptable to set boundaries around how much external influence you allow in your life.

Being able to sift through advice helps you maintain your identity while benefiting from the insights of others.

How to Take Criticism Constructively

Receiving criticism can be uncomfortable, but it's an integral part of growth.

- **Developing a Thick Skin**: Learning to differentiate between constructive criticism and personal attacks is essential. Understand that constructive feedback is meant to help you improve, not to diminish your worth.

- **Practice Gratitude**: When receiving criticism, express gratitude for the feedback. This simple act can shift your mindset from defensiveness to openness. For instance, saying "Thank you for your input; I appreciate your perspective" can create a positive atmosphere for further discussion.

Embracing criticism as a valuable tool can significantly enhance your personal and professional development.

Identifying Advice That's Worth Trying

With the digital age offering an overwhelming amount of information, discerning what advice is genuinely worth your attention is paramount.

- **Conducting Research**: Before implementing advice, do some research. Check the credibility of the source and look for testimonials or case studies that validate the effectiveness of the advice. This process can help you separate valuable insights from misleading information.

- **Trial and Error**: Sometimes, the only way to know if advice is beneficial is to try it out. Start small—experiment with different approaches to see what resonates best with your situation.

By developing a critical approach to advice, you empower yourself to make informed decisions that align with your goals.

Balancing Openness with Self-Confidence

Navigating the complex landscape of advice requires both openness to new ideas and a solid sense of self-confidence.

- **Affirming Your Values**: Stay grounded in your core beliefs and values. This self-awareness enables you to filter advice effectively and adopt strategies that align with your vision.

- **Fostering a Growth Mindset**: Embrace challenges as opportunities for growth. When you approach advice with a mindset geared toward learning and development, you can remain open to new ideas while still trusting your instincts.

Balancing these aspects enhances your ability to engage in meaningful discussions and make sound decisions.

The Future of Advice: Learning in the Digital Age

As we move further into the digital age, the landscape of advice-giving and receiving continues to evolve. The internet has made advice more accessible than ever, but it also complicates the process.

- **Navigating the Information Overload**: With countless sources of information, it's crucial to develop critical thinking skills. Cultivate your ability to assess the reliability of sources and discern which advice aligns with your situation.

- **Harnessing Digital Tools**: Use online resources such as forums, webinars, and courses to broaden your knowledge base. Engaging with diverse perspectives can enrich your understanding and provide you with valuable insights.

As we adapt to the changing dynamics of communication, let's commit to becoming more discerning consumers of advice.

Why It's Okay to Be Wrong and Learn from It

No one is infallible, and acknowledging this truth can liberate us from the pressure of perfection.

- **Reframing Failure**: Instead of viewing failure as a negative outcome, consider it an opportunity for growth. Reflect on what went wrong, extract the lessons, and use that knowledge to inform your future decisions.

- **Sharing Vulnerability**: Sharing your experiences of failure can create a culture of openness. When we acknowledge our missteps, we encourage others to do the same, fostering an environment where everyone feels safe to learn and grow.

Embracing the reality of mistakes as part of the journey can strengthen your resilience and adaptability.

Curating Your Personal Learning Network

Your personal learning network can significantly influence the quality of advice you receive.

- **Engage with Diverse Voices**: Surround yourself with individuals who bring varied experiences and perspectives. This diversity enhances your understanding and exposes you to new ideas.

- **Active Participation**: Take an active role in your network. Engage in discussions, share insights, and contribute to the collective knowledge. This engagement not only enriches your learning experience but also strengthens relationships.

Understanding the Limits of Your Experience

When offering advice, it's essential to acknowledge the limits of your own experiences. Many people fall into the trap of believing their journey is a universal template. However, this belief can lead to advice that feels dismissive or irrelevant to others.

- **Contextual Awareness**: Every person's journey is shaped by a myriad of factors, including background, culture, and personal circumstances. Recognizing this diversity is crucial in providing valuable advice. For instance, a piece of career advice that worked well for you might not be applicable to someone in a different industry or facing distinct challenges. The impact of one's environment—be it familial, socio-economic, or cultural—can drastically alter how advice is received and implemented. Tailoring advice to consider these differences can make it more relatable and effective.

- **The Dunning-Kruger Effect**: This cognitive bias occurs when individuals with limited knowledge in a domain overestimate their expertise. Being aware of this tendency can help you stay humble and approach advice-giving with a healthy dose of skepticism about your own capabilities. The more you recognize your limitations, the more you open yourself up to learning from others as well.

By understanding the limits of your experience, you not only improve the quality of the advice you provide but also create an atmosphere of mutual respect and learning.

The Importance of Listening Before Speaking

Active listening is one of the most powerful tools in effective communication. It lays the foundation for meaningful advice exchange.

- **The Power of Non-Verbal Cues**: Pay attention to the speaker's body language and tone. Sometimes, what isn't said can be just as important as the words spoken. Non-verbal cues can reveal underlying emotions or concerns that may be essential for you to consider before offering advice. This attentiveness allows you to respond more thoughtfully and meaningfully.

- **Refrain from Interrupting**: Allow the person to express their thoughts fully before you respond. Interruptions can make individuals feel undervalued, and it might prevent you from fully grasping their perspective. Practicing patience during conversations not only enhances understanding but also establishes trust.

Engaging in this way cultivates trust and encourages deeper conversations. The more you listen, the more insightful your advice will become.

Building Empathy in Conversations

Empathy is at the heart of effective communication. It allows you to connect with others on a deeper level, fostering a sense of safety and openness in the conversation.

- **Practice Reflective Listening**: After someone shares their story or problem, summarize what you've heard and reflect it back to them. This not only demonstrates that you're actively listening but also helps clarify any misunderstandings. For example, you might say, "It sounds like you're feeling overwhelmed because of X situation. Is that right?" This approach invites further dialogue and shows that you genuinely care about their feelings.

- **Avoid Judgment**: Approach every conversation without preconceived notions or judgments. Everyone's experiences are valid, and by suspending your judgment, you create a safe space for sharing. This non-judgmental approach encourages openness, allowing the person to share their feelings and experiences more freely.

Building empathy doesn't just enrich the advice-giving experience; it transforms it into a collaborative process where both parties can learn and grow.

Learning to Receive Advice Without Losing Yourself

The flip side of giving advice is receiving it. Often, this can feel daunting, especially if the advice challenges your current beliefs or practices.

- **Assessing Value**: Not all advice will resonate with you, and that's perfectly okay. Cultivating the ability to discern which pieces of advice align with your values and aspirations is vital. As you evaluate advice, consider the source, the context, and how it relates to your own experiences. Acknowledging that some advice may not be applicable to your situation empowers you to make decisions that are right for you.

- **Setting Boundaries**: While it's beneficial to be open to advice, it's equally important to know your limits. If advice feels misaligned with your core values, it's perfectly acceptable to set boundaries around how much external influence you allow in your life. This self-awareness helps you protect your individuality while still benefiting from external insights.

Being able to sift through advice helps you maintain your identity while benefiting from the insights of others.

How to Take Criticism Constructively

Receiving criticism can be uncomfortable, but it's an integral part of growth.

- **Developing a Thick Skin**: Learning to differentiate between constructive criticism and personal attacks is essential. Understand that constructive feedback is meant to help you improve, not to diminish your worth. This differentiation allows you to embrace feedback without taking it personally.

- **Practice Gratitude**: When receiving criticism, express gratitude for the feedback. This simple act can shift your mindset from defensiveness to openness. For instance, saying "Thank you for your input; I appreciate your perspective" can create a positive atmosphere for further discussion. This practice not only enhances your resilience but also encourages a culture of mutual respect in your interactions.

Embracing criticism as a valuable tool can significantly enhance your personal and professional development.

Identifying Advice That's Worth Trying

With the digital age offering an overwhelming amount of information, discerning what advice is genuinely worth your attention is paramount.

- **Conducting Research**: Before implementing advice, do some research. Check the credibility of the source and look for testimonials or case studies that validate the effectiveness of the advice. This process can help you separate valuable insights from misleading information.

- **Trial and Error**: Sometimes, the only way to know if advice is beneficial is to try it out. Start small—experiment with different approaches to see what resonates best with your situation. Documenting your experiences can also help you assess what works and what doesn't, giving you a more informed basis for future decisions.

By developing a critical approach to advice, you empower yourself to make informed decisions that align with your goals.

Balancing Openness with Self-Confidence

Navigating the complex landscape of advice requires both openness to new ideas and a solid sense of self-confidence.

- **Affirming Your Values**: Stay grounded in your core beliefs and values. This self-awareness enables you to filter advice effectively and adopt strategies that align with your vision. A strong sense of self can act as an anchor when faced with conflicting opinions or advice that doesn't resonate with you.

- **Fostering a Growth Mindset**: Embrace challenges as opportunities for growth. When you approach advice with a mindset geared toward learning and development, you can remain open to new ideas while still trusting your instincts. This balance allows you to engage with advice critically without shutting down valuable insights.

Balancing these aspects enhances your ability to engage in meaningful discussions and make sound decisions.

The Future of Advice: Learning in the Digital Age

As we move further into the digital age, the landscape of advice-giving and receiving continues to evolve. The internet has made advice more accessible than ever, but it also complicates the process.

- **Navigating the Information Overload**: With countless sources of information, it's crucial to develop critical thinking skills. Cultivate your ability to assess the reliability of sources and discern which advice aligns with your situation. Understanding how to evaluate information critically will serve you well in both personal and professional contexts.

- **Harnessing Digital Tools**: Use online resources such as forums, webinars, and courses to broaden your knowledge base. Engaging with diverse perspectives can enrich your understanding and provide you with valuable insights. Social media platforms can also be beneficial for connecting with mentors and like-minded individuals who can offer guidance and support.

As we adapt to the changing dynamics of communication, let's commit to becoming more discerning consumers of advice.

Why It's Okay to Be Wrong and Learn from It

No one is infallible, and acknowledging this truth can liberate us from the pressure of perfection.

- **Reframing Failure**: Instead of viewing failure as a negative outcome, consider it an opportunity for growth. Reflect on what went wrong, extract the lessons, and use that knowledge to inform your future decisions. This reflective practice can transform setbacks into powerful learning experiences.

- **Sharing Vulnerability**: Sharing your experiences of failure can create a culture of openness. When we acknowledge our missteps, we encourage others to do the same, fostering an environment where everyone feels safe to learn and grow. This vulnerability can also strengthen relationships and build trust, as people appreciate authenticity and honesty.

Embracing the reality of mistakes as part of the journey can strengthen your resilience and adaptability.

Curating Your Personal Learning Network

Your personal learning network can significantly influence the quality of advice you receive.

- **Engage with Diverse Voices**: Surround yourself with individuals who bring varied experiences and perspectives. This diversity enhances your understanding and exposes you to new ideas. By engaging with people from different backgrounds, you can challenge your assumptions and broaden your horizons.

- **Active Participation**: Take an active role in your network. Engage in discussions, share insights, and contribute to the collective knowledge. This engagement not only enriches your learning experience but also strengthens relationships. Being an active participant encourages reciprocity, where others will also be inclined to share their knowledge and experiences.

Understanding the Limits of Your Experience

When offering advice, it's essential to acknowledge the limits of your own experiences. Many people fall into the trap of believing their journey is a universal template. However, this belief can lead to advice that feels dismissive or irrelevant to others.

- **Contextual Awareness**: Every person's journey is shaped by a myriad of factors, including background, culture, and personal circumstances. Recognizing this diversity is crucial in providing valuable advice. For instance, a piece of career advice that worked well for you might not be applicable to someone in a different industry or facing distinct challenges. The impact of one's environment—be it familial, socio-economic, or cultural—can drastically alter how advice is received and implemented. Tailoring advice to consider these differences can make it more relatable and effective.

- **The Dunning-Kruger Effect**: This cognitive bias occurs when individuals with limited knowledge in a domain overestimate their expertise. Being aware of this tendency can help you stay humble and approach advice-giving with a healthy dose of skepticism about your own capabilities. The more you recognize your limitations, the more you open yourself up to learning from others as well.

By understanding the limits of your experience, you not only improve the quality of the advice you provide but also create an atmosphere of mutual respect and learning.

The Importance of Listening Before Speaking

Active listening is one of the most powerful tools in effective communication. It lays the foundation for meaningful advice exchange.

- **The Power of Non-Verbal Cues**: Pay attention to the speaker's body language and tone. Sometimes, what isn't said can be just as important as the words spoken. Non-verbal cues can reveal underlying emotions or concerns that may be essential for you to consider before offering advice. This attentiveness allows you to respond more thoughtfully and meaningfully.

- **Refrain from Interrupting**: Allow the person to express their thoughts fully before you respond. Interruptions can make individuals feel undervalued, and it might prevent you from fully grasping their perspective. Practicing patience during conversations not only enhances understanding but also establishes trust.

Engaging in this way cultivates trust and encourages deeper conversations. The more you listen, the more insightful your advice will become.

Building Empathy in Conversations

Empathy is at the heart of effective communication. It allows you to connect with others on a deeper level, fostering a sense of safety and openness in the conversation.

- **Practice Reflective Listening**: After someone shares their story or problem, summarize what you've heard and reflect it back to them. This not only demonstrates that you're actively listening but also helps clarify any misunderstandings. For example, you might say, "It sounds like you're feeling overwhelmed because of X situation. Is that right?" This approach invites further dialogue and shows that you genuinely care about their feelings and thoughts.

- **Avoid Judgment**: Approach every conversation without preconceived notions or judgments. Everyone's experiences are valid, and by suspending your judgment, you create a safe space for sharing. This non-judgmental approach encourages openness, allowing the person to share their feelings and experiences more freely.

Building empathy doesn't just enrich the advice-giving experience; it transforms it into a collaborative process where both parties can learn and grow.

Learning to Receive Advice Without Losing Yourself

The flip side of giving advice is receiving it. Often, this can feel daunting, especially if the advice challenges your current beliefs or practices.

- **Assessing Value**: Not all advice will resonate with you, and that's perfectly okay. Cultivating the ability to discern which pieces of advice align with your values and aspirations is vital. As you evaluate advice, consider the source, the context, and how it relates to your own experiences. Acknowledging that some advice may not be applicable to your situation empowers you to make decisions that are right for you.

- **Setting Boundaries**: While it's beneficial to be open to advice, it's equally important to know your limits. If advice feels misaligned with your core values, it's perfectly acceptable to set boundaries around how much external influence you allow in your life. This self-awareness helps you protect your individuality while still benefiting from external insights.

Being able to sift through advice helps you maintain your identity while benefiting from the insights of others.

How to Take Criticism Constructively

Receiving criticism can be uncomfortable, but it's an integral part of growth.

- **Developing a Thick Skin**: Learning to differentiate between constructive criticism and personal attacks is essential. Understand that constructive feedback is meant to help you improve, not to diminish your worth. This differentiation allows you to embrace feedback without taking it personally.

- **Practice Gratitude**: When receiving criticism, express gratitude for the feedback. This simple act can shift your mindset from defensiveness to openness. For instance, saying "Thank you for your input; I appreciate your perspective" can create a positive atmosphere for further discussion. This practice not only enhances your resilience but also encourages a culture of mutual respect in your interactions.

Embracing criticism as a valuable tool can significantly enhance your personal and professional development.

Identifying Advice That's Worth Trying

With the digital age offering an overwhelming amount of information, discerning what advice is genuinely worth your attention is paramount.

- **Conducting Research**: Before implementing advice, do some research. Check the credibility of the source and look for testimonials or case studies that validate the effectiveness of the advice. This process can help you separate valuable insights from misleading information.

- **Trial and Error**: Sometimes, the only way to know if advice is beneficial is to try it out. Start small—experiment with different approaches to see what resonates best with your situation. Documenting your experiences can also help you assess what works and what doesn't, giving you a more informed basis for future decisions.

By developing a critical approach to advice, you empower yourself to make informed decisions that align with your goals.

Balancing Openness with Self-Confidence

Navigating the complex landscape of advice requires both openness to new ideas and a solid sense of self-confidence.

- **Affirming Your Values**: Stay grounded in your core beliefs and values. This self-awareness enables you to filter advice effectively and adopt strategies that align with your vision. A strong sense of self can act as an anchor when faced with conflicting opinions or advice that doesn't resonate with you.

- **Fostering a Growth Mindset**: Embrace challenges as opportunities for growth. When you approach advice with a mindset geared toward learning and development, you can remain open to new ideas while still trusting your instincts. This balance allows you to engage with advice critically without shutting down valuable insights.

Balancing these aspects enhances your ability to engage in meaningful discussions and make sound decisions.

The Future of Advice: Learning in the Digital Age

As we move further into the digital age, the landscape of advice-giving and receiving continues to evolve. The internet has made advice more accessible than ever, but it also complicates the process.

- **Navigating the Information Overload**: With countless sources of information, it's crucial to develop critical thinking skills. Cultivate your ability to assess the reliability of sources and discern which advice aligns with your situation. Understanding how to evaluate information critically will serve you well in both personal and professional contexts.

- **Harnessing Digital Tools**: Use online resources such as forums, webinars, and courses to broaden your knowledge base. Engaging with diverse perspectives can enrich your understanding and provide you with valuable insights. Social media platforms can also be beneficial for connecting with mentors and like-minded individuals who can offer guidance and support.

As we adapt to the changing dynamics of communication, let's commit to becoming more discerning consumers of advice.

Why It's Okay to Be Wrong and Learn from It

No one is infallible, and acknowledging this truth can liberate us from the pressure of perfection.

- **Reframing Failure**: Instead of viewing failure as a negative outcome, consider it an opportunity for growth. Reflect on what went wrong, extract the lessons, and use that knowledge to inform your future decisions. This reflective practice can transform setbacks into powerful learning experiences.

- **Sharing Vulnerability**: Sharing your experiences of failure can create a culture of openness. When we acknowledge our missteps, we encourage others to do the same, fostering an environment where everyone feels safe to learn and grow. This vulnerability can also strengthen relationships and build trust, as people appreciate authenticity and honesty.

Embracing the reality of mistakes as part of the journey can strengthen your resilience and adaptability.

Curating Your Personal Learning Network

Your personal learning network can significantly influence the quality of advice you receive.

- **Engage with Diverse Voices**: Surround yourself with individuals who bring varied experiences and perspectives. This diversity enhances your understanding and exposes you to new ideas. By engaging with people from different backgrounds, you can challenge your assumptions and broaden your horizons.

- **Active Participation**: Take an active role in your network. Engage in discussions, share insights, and contribute to the collective knowledge. This engagement not only enriches your learning experience but also strengthens relationships. Being an active participant encourages reciprocity, where others will also be inclined to share their knowledge and experiences.

By curating a dynamic learning network, you position yourself for continual growth and adaptation.

The Role of Mentorship

Mentorship is a powerful tool in the realm of advice.

- **Finding the Right Mentor**: Seek mentors who resonate with your values and aspirations. A mentor should not only offer guidance but also challenge you to think critically and develop your skills. The mentor-mentee relationship thrives on mutual respect and open communication, making it essential to find someone who understands your journey.

- **Giving Back**: As you grow and gain experience, consider becoming a mentor yourself. Sharing your knowledge and experiences can be incredibly rewarding. Mentorship allows you to reflect on your journey, reinforce your learning, and contribute to someone else's growth.

As we reach the end of this exploration into the art of giving and receiving advice, it's important to reflect on the journey we've undertaken together. Throughout this chapter, we have delved into the multifaceted nature of advice, recognizing that it is not just about the information exchanged but also about the connections forged in the process.

The ability to give advice effectively, without coming across as a know-it-all, requires a deep understanding of our limitations and a commitment to active listening. Empathy is not merely a tool but a fundamental aspect of meaningful conversations that foster mutual growth.

On the flip side, receiving advice is an equally important skill. It involves discernment, vulnerability, and the courage to accept that we don't have all the answers. By learning to take criticism constructively and identifying what advice aligns with our values, we can navigate the complexities of personal and professional development with confidence.

In an age saturated with information, curating our personal learning networks and remaining open to diverse perspectives can significantly enhance our journey. It's vital to recognize that making mistakes and learning from them is part of growth. The ability to embrace our imperfections and view them as opportunities for learning strengthens our resilience.

As we close this chapter and the book, let us carry forward the principles of empathy, respect, and openness in our advice exchanges.

Each interaction is an opportunity to learn, grow, and connect with others, enriching our lives and the lives of those around us.

Final Thoughts

The journey of personal development is ongoing, and the lessons we've shared here are just the beginning. As you navigate the complexities of giving and receiving advice in your own life, remember to be patient with yourself and others. Growth takes time, and every step forward, no matter how small, is significant.

Embrace the unique tapestry of experiences that each person brings to the table. By doing so, we cultivate a culture of support and understanding, where advice becomes a collaborative process rather than a one-sided exchange. Let's strive to create environments—be it at work, home, or within our communities—where conversations thrive on respect, empathy, and the genuine desire to uplift one another.

Thank you for joining me on this journey. May your future interactions be filled with wisdom, growth, and meaningful connections as you navigate the beautiful complexities of life. Keep learning, keep sharing, and most importantly, keep being open to the advice that comes your way, for it holds the potential to transform your journey in unexpected and profound ways.

Thank You

Milton Keynes UK
Ingram Content Group UK Ltd.
UKHW021925281024
450365UK00017B/972